This Book Is Expensive

I0460799

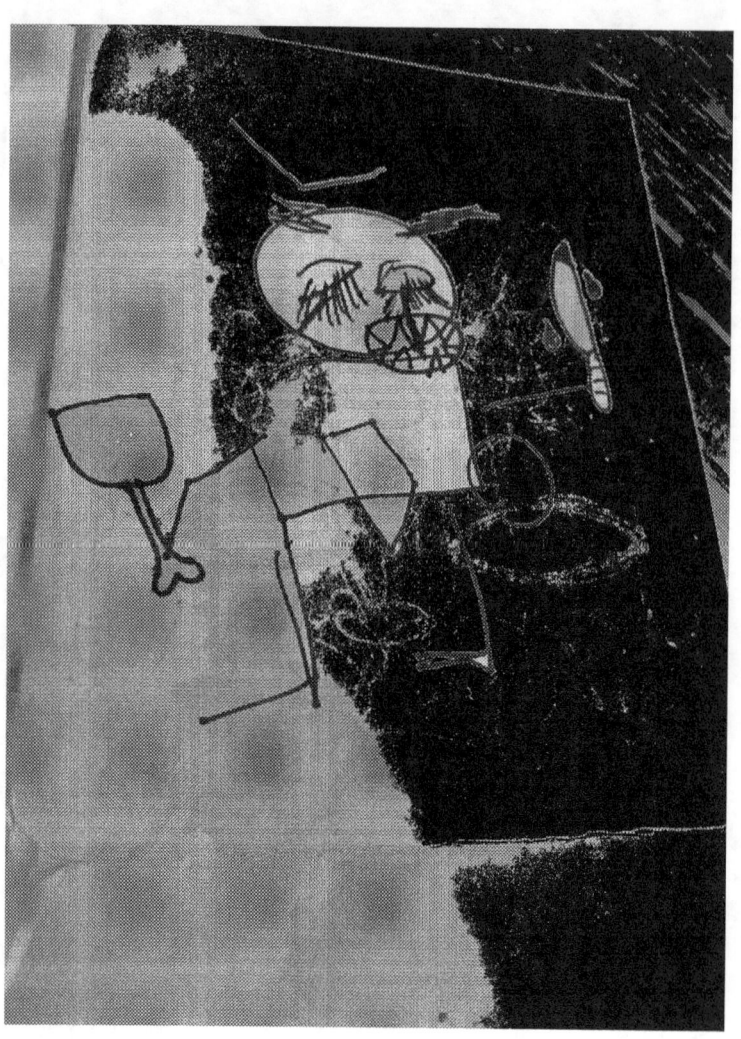

This Book Is Expensive

A

Poetic   Experience

By

Nick Oliveri

You're welcome.

A

Poetic   Experience

By

Nick Oliveri

Heed a genius.
Read His secrets.

You pushed me to the reaches,
Now I have to reveal it.

This book is expensive,
Yet I know you'll feel it.

I know you'll feel it.

Trigger Warning:

Ill-advised drug abuse
Explicit language use
Religious figures mentioned irreverently
Potential political discussion flippantly
Tobacco and alcohol glorified messily
Mentioning of an intelligence agency
Sexual assault (maybe)
The "r" word (rape)
General irreverence toward sacred institutions
The other "r" word (retard)
Famous names mentioned (no relation to anyone
alive or dead, or any persons ever existing)
A general disregard for social conventions
Elitist rhetoric
Anti-male sentiment
Veiled misogyny
Blatant misogyny
Pleas for monogamy
Abrahamic religions praised
Abrahamic religions exalted
Nihilism
Sexism
White male rage
Classicism
The "g" word (God)
Prayer
Praise for the matriarchy
Benzodiazepines
Companies mentioned (strictly coincidentally)
Appreciation for females

The "m" word (moron)
The "c" word (crazy)
Narcissism
Self-doubt
Suicide
Depictions of Baby Jesus
Praise for females
Violence
Assault and battery
Mentionings of "PTSD"
Psychological exploration
Objectification of women
Violence towards men
Equal opportunism
Assertions about the afterlife
Offensive vagaries
Lies
Irreverence toward Buddhism
Truth
Dark emotions
Hope
Lack of Anti-Trump sentiment
Fraternity brothers preparing for death
Russo-Ukrainian war
The word "rapist"
Death and grief
Depictions of The Virgin Mary
Antisemitism
Pro-Jewish Sentiment
Monarchism
Zionism
Fun musings and poems of new adventure

Loneliness
Longing
Sadness
Crude drawings of stick figures with knives
Crude drawings of stick figures and suicide
Goya's Black Paintings
Hope
Smoking and more drug use
Positivity in the face of the world's ills
Women getting their doctorate
Stuffy literary critics
Immolation and burning flesh
Guns and gun violence
Lack of silence
Heartbreak
Orphans
Existentialism
Coarse language
Murder
The "m" word (Muhammad)
The "m" word (Mohamed)
Superiority complexes
Inferiority complexes
Torture
Self-righteousness
Slavery
Ableist language
Genocide

Reader and listener discretion is advised.

Now I'm done with conventions—
Fed up with inventions.
What more is there to make?
Could there be such a quest?

I save my message for the rest.

Sincerely,
Enjoy the show and the mess,
Yours Truly,

The Best

Dedication

I dedicate this book to me:
The greatest artist to spit on dirt;
The greatest writer to piss on earth—
The same one who already did it all.

So, this is my dedication,
My so-public self-immolation,
My destructive imitation
Of those before my earth's invitation,
After I learned I had no limitations—
Before I learn there are no secrets;
Before my PTSD goes on vacation.

I dedicate this to me.
That's who wrote it, after all:
Me
Nick Oliveri
The same one who doubted me
Was always who had the key,
The one who encouraged me—
The lone figure in purgatory
The only
Nick Oliveri
Me, simply me:
Nick Oliveri

I composed this all for free.
And now you've paid the fee.
I dedicate this to me,
Nick Oliveri

The young man who varies
In mood and is very
Tempestuous in mood;
Rife with strife and aloof.
To me:
Nick Oliveri

The dawn of Man
Rises again
Humanity finally has found
An extraterrestrial friend.

The End.

Thanks again.

Prologue

"This guy's a dilettante. How could think he's the best when he's never read Eliot, Carroll, or Carole?"

"Well, he could've read them, but those are popular ones.... I mean figures like Pushkin, Barrow, or Woolf."

"Agreed. He's never read the classics yet is selling this for dough."

"That's exactly my point, though! This kid doesn't know about Ancient Greats or Sappho—he couldn't possibly know. The criticism will pan out. I'm learning about them in class right now."

"The critics will pan it."

"Such a loser to think he could overshadow all those greats.... Why would you even write poetry? We have ChatGPT!"

"It's a big promise without bringing much of anything; he should just get over his mistakes.... Like, we all have sad feelings! Dude, get over it. We all go through those things but don't need to share them unlike that wannabe—Nick Oliveri."

"Hey....
Hey, man, you good? You look a little pale."

"I just… it's nothing. I'm fine, man."

"You sure?"

"Yeah, I guess so."

"Aright. Have a good night."

"It's just—real quick—are our…uhh…are our—"

"Just spit it out, bro."

"Are our words being manipulated by him?"

"What do you mean?"

"Like manipulated by him, in stipulated poems, contrived by human mind's creations. Like, I just—"

"Yo, dude…. You need to get some rest. You're overthinking. You need to chill. Is that…. What's wrong?"

"Nothing. I just feel like I'm part of a song."

"Like lyrics?"

"Think I just need my bong."

"But you're not a product, right?"

"I don't think he would ever make art for profit stuff."

"So he can't be that tough."

"But who is he? I think we're figments, man! Don't you see? All we've been is indignant—damn!"

"Dude, get your hands off me!"

"I swear he's doing this!"

"What are you looking at?"

"He's, he's everywhere. Don't you get that?"

"Is he in the same place we're at?"

"He's creating us while we chat!"

"Holy.... So you mean that—"

"Yes, man! He's contriving our every thought and word with a pen."

"Don't be scared.... He doesn't know the classics like Shakespeare and them."

"No, your fear should be real! He knows our actions and all about King Lear and your brother's eyes. Don't you see?"

"Well, my eyes are wide…. Also, my older brother died."

"If he wished, I think he could kill us with a lie."

"But if he created us, then why cry?"

"He made us—college kids in a poem…. Our existence is only alive as his pen."

"It's fragile as life itself, then."

"He could make us 'has-beens.'"

"But what about all the messages I send—that my sister sends? Her, too? What about the rest of our friends?"

"He created us and her, too. It's reality he bends."

"Then I take back all I said."

"It doesn't matter; now we're dead."

"Then it's been a good run, Ben."

"Dude, holding my hand won't stop his pen."

"Is there something to him we could lend?"

"No, I don't think so—he's like God from the old testament. All we can do is try to repent. I don't see any mercy that he could send."

"Then... this is where our story ends."

"I love you, man."

"Me too, but his name will forever ring. We are mere contrivances of a single mind."

"Then it's been a good run, though we may be in a bind."

"In this page, we'll at least live forever as flat-scared characters."

"But isn't this too experimental for a single writer?"

"If our story ends here, let's just sit and sip that hard cider in the fridge."

"Jeez. Don't you think that's cheesy?"

"Doesn't matter; for him, it's easy."

"But how could it be so breezy?"

"Because he can create the wind."

"Could he absolve me of my sins?"

"I don't know.... I think so, with grace in dim—"

"Tell me! Could he forgive me if he created me?"

"Lay off, man. Chill. Why would he forsake if he created thee?"

"Why are we now speaking in desperate pleas?"

"Because he created you and contrived me as well—don't you see?"

"I just hope he forgives me."

"Doth matter if created by thee?"

"Could you please repeat?"

"Doth *it* matter... if you were created by He?"

"I don't know, actually."

This Book Is Expensive

But

What would you pay

For one thousand lifetimes?

Though lawyers are expensive, I was repeatedly told
By an attorney named Altman or Silverman
That this work's not sponsored by any one man
Other than I, the artist to rebuke legalists
Bearing all the sins the {censored} never would've
Finding in their greedy ids
To take responsibility in fits
For pathologies I cannot control.

I am beginning to think my legal counsel
Does not care about my struggle
And that may possibly be fair—
For they know I care not for theirs.

You know what I mean.
This world has to be divided.
This world has to be divided.
If you think Heaven can live on Earth,
Then you are simply misguided.

This ride with its ups and downs provided
Will show you exactly why,
Or, maybe, mere snapshot in time—
A boy's petulant attempt... to rhyme?

Blame it all on them,
Just not their sacred cow;
My attorney just quit for now.
I may have to change my plans,

Though I do think it rather odd
That a Protestant warned me

Not to say the word, "Mossad."

Let my written pictures entertain thee.

Don't speak too loud.
Don't say what is disallowed.
Don't reveal intelligence.
Just take it as evidence.
Take what you can and give nothing back.
Go and live and run and bleed and see
The rose-red, flamingo-pink rage.
Life is no teacher or sage.
Life is but a plaything—
Tear its fleshy seams,
Abuse it,
Use it,
Never recuse it.
Either way
You will lose it.

Welcome To The Jungle Part 1

Welcome to the jungle
Where the hungry eat the humble
They're only gonna' want you
When they can't have you
They're only gonna' leave
When they don't need you
The jungle onwardly thrives;
The greatest machine never created
It is only death to stay alive
Life is killing to survive
Slowly die
Slowly die
Quickly cry and move on toward killing

Oh, welcome to the jungle
Where the hungry eat the humble
And unseen sounds abound!
Slithering, tiny taps as steps
Of spindly insects
Tigers stalk and monkeys mumble
Where Resolve melts
And Willpower crumbles
Where the soulless survive for
Just one
More
Moment

Wicked eyes see the world
Righteous eyes die in light
Shaded by canopy's blinding plight

Raided by rapists wanting your life

Welcome to the jungle.

Welcome to the house of horrors
The endless landscape
The throng of tools and trees
The barrels of ghouls and bees
Stingers ease when hurt looms tall
Bringing means of death delivery
To all

So, welcome to the jungle
A place where you can't be humble
Or have to be, possibly
If you have no means of killing me
It's a place where the angry reign
Only clouds cover sky
Only empty stomachs, only rain
Welcome to the jungle
To the many domains of pain
All that is lost is a gain
Welcome to the clean coat stained
The mosquito suckling real red
While you wind up pale and dead
The boy is taking real meds
The jungle is a living deathbed
I swear it!

Writhing with restless souls
And single-minded slitted eyes
With singular goals

You've already paid the toll
There must
Be life
After
Death
Because it seems
As though
You're already
Dead.
Welcome.

Welcome to the jungle.

Welcome To The Jungle Part (Epilogue)

"Oh my God! Did that male poet just write 'rapist?'"

"I think he did. And he didn't even give a trigger warning!"

"So he's sexist and offensive? His work shouldn't be seen."

"He's such a scumbag and angry and mean...."

"Then we'll leave him without anything!"

"We'll cancel him and smear him. He'll be left with nothing."

"To bury him, we'll use every means!"

"He said a bad word and wrote gory scenes."

"I know. He's literally disgusting."

"We will bring him to justice—you and me."

"And once we take everything, we will be free."

"Without men like him—a better society!"

"I'm so glad we think similarly;

For you, I would do anything!"

"Can I borrow ten dollars, please?"

"Uhm, no, sorry.... It's a tough economy."

You Get Another Chance Today

And the sun rises
Or it also rises
As Hemingway said
Literary allusions
Are always illusory
To dreary me

Please, gold ray pike blue skies
On a new, a brighter day
A new breath quiet
A single blink silent
Over the hills and far away
You get another chance today

Poem 89

If I had two loves to give,
I'd surely give up three.
One is far too many
And two is one too free.
Until the joy escapes me
And soon the tears follow the glee.
I write this in the dark.

Maybe you can relate to me.

Love is like a forest lost,
Sand spacious mounds,
Or a poem found;
Love is the deepest pit
Gashing deeply dead ground.

It tickles and give us glee.
I give so much for free;
I want it to be you and me
All my love for you, but, then again,
Maybe
I've given too much love to thee.
Now, they ask,
"Is there a poem ninety?"
They always want more from me.

Winter Killed His Steed

I reside comfortably at
Both ends of the spear
I can attack and defend
And hold up the weight of the blade
Though the double-sided demon lurks
When I write this at dawn.
What else would I do with this pain?
God-willing, me alone, cradle to knave

Heavy footsteps make long campaigns
I am him; I am He who took the reigns

Oh, but my ride broke down;
My steed lost its last breath,
Huffing, huffing, then death.
Its wild eyes went dim.
It gasped hurried, hallowed breaths
Shallow death in deep snow
I pet my steed for the last time.

My valiant stallion to task
My venture once bested by fate
twice bested too late
And
So on
And so it goes.

The winds blow stronger.
I travel farther, going longer
Than my feet can carry me

As my chest beats for a break in
Cold desert sands empty.
No soul to speak to;
And the winds blow colder yet
Bitter bone-chilling threat
Without my steed, I race to death

Battle up the hill,
For what gain I do not know.
I miss my horse's shrill;
I hark the past's woe

Flakes become wet and heavy
The sand sinks quicker now
The skies open up and laugh
The Matriarch's taken throne, alas
No one is coming home
There is no vitriol; my lungs turn cold
The spirits of a wind unknown
But to carry on is all I know
The twine of my torso was not made in vain
Feet, don't fail, stay faithful; deliver me.

Conjured devils preying upon ill measures
Met with grit teeth, but he stays
One step ahead
I abandoned you long ago
Yet you stay in my head
Yet I smell you in my bed
A wrangled mess of sheets
The devil wanted it to be
He mocks me mercilessly

He mocks me mercilessly
Upon illusions too real
Pale bodies lie endlessly

I carry onward
But I stop at the past
And think, and dream
And reminisce about actions rash
Picturing better days
Now those pictures lie in my way
Upon my gaze opaque

My mother told me
She wants to take the pain away.
I said, "what do you mean?"

"I wish you didn't have to face it."

"I fucking do, so save it."

She just wants me to be normal
Sleep and be calm and be cordial,
But when she cries,
'Tis only pain dripping from her eyes.
I carry all the burden otherwise.
Toxic lies, bad eyes, poor life of the wanderer who
Bargains with no one now
For he's been stolen from, taken, beaten
Into the sands he goes, wriggling for a light
But only the night shows
New means of plight

"Why is there so much hurt?"

But the sands come to eat him.
The bandits come to hack his neck
He needed somebody
He needed a certain somebody
To save him from his recklessness
But a kid has no say, only petulance

The winds howl
The sands pile
Cold snow wiles
There is no dawn
No holding on
Foreboding guile
Of the boy who drank the sand
And lay lifeless beneath the snow
Beneath thin ice
Surrounded by powder
A freezing body lies
Black eyes
Blue lips
Open mouth receives an avalanche
The snow-cold brittle time
Withering lungs like coal mines;
Decaying brains are gold mines
For profit and profit seekers.

Oh, though,

With his steed now dead,

In the cold gray endless
There must be a way to
Ramble on
Beneath this wily madness
There was a story to tell thee
I swear, there always will be.

Though his steed died
And the road is endless
And the lights are few and far,
There is a spark.
Hark!
There is a story to live.

I Am A God

I am Scorsese
And I am the sum of his films
All in all: I am bin Talal
I am his gold and holdings and secret twat
Hark! I am Basquiat
And the canvas on which he spills
I am Napoleon
And two-thirds of Moscow burning
I am Western Europe learning
Of a disaster mine
So then twenty-first century minds
Can feel the need to opine empty motto
But I am all of their unearned bravado
And a skinny big lips' Moscato
And all the cultures I don't know.

I am Fear.
I am he who wrote King Lear.
I am The Aztec's final spear.

I'm what Pollock tried
Michelangelo divined
I'm as stupid as Einstein
Try to keep that in mind.

I am Lana's 13 Beaches
I am the pen of Nietzsche's
I am Hannibal of Carthage
Over the hills and far away
Breaches, sieges, and war elephants

Oh, now I think I'm Led Zeppelin
I'm Weezy, I'm Jeezy, I'm Ye or Nietzsche
I'm Mike Tyson in his prime
Randy Johnson glaring on high

I'm Steve Irwin before the stingray
I am Poison and Sting, singing aloud
I am Tom Brady silencing hostile crowds
Nabokov would blush at this literary sound,
And Virginia Woolf of Hogarth proud.
For I am both of them; I am all of them
Hemingway and Thompson abound
In fast diction with less punctuation

I'm every beat writer with
More mess, less buddies;
I'm a song of Scott Mescudi's.
I am my unborn son
I count myself as one
I'm Cartman committing arson
I am South Park
I'm Rodman catching more charges
Than Steve Largent—also me
And I am also He

I am every child cold and lonely
I am all parents without custody
I am Samson in The Book
Look at me now, Delilah:
I'm ev'ry step the Buddha took
I also wrote Siddhartha
And I have Herman Hesse's Nobel Prize

I'm the zombie king, the smoothie king
The corporate shill and Martin Luther's King
I am Malcolm X's lucid dream
I'm what they told me not to be
And I am thee; but you are not me
See, I am Salvator Mundi;
The auction and Christie's fee
And I am Da Vinci
I am absolutely most of the time never free
Because I am De Medici
Also, the Rothschild family.
I rule the world and have enslaved thee.
I am Greed and every banker
Mansa Musa's insolent trek
Slavery and finance;
Synonymous dance.
I am England; I am France
I am the Zulu King
Whose name is not parlance

I'm both smoke and clean air
Now I'm Robespierre
And the guillotine
And Antoinette's brassiere
I am Beethoven's ear
And I was Van Gogh crying
Now I'm Cobain dying
Remnants of a brain lying

I am Jimi, Jimmy, and C.S. Snow
Alan Page and Reggie White with more to go
I've been everywhere with nowhere to go

I'm your schoolyard bully and your trauma
Ronaldo, Messi, and to rhyme: Obama
Yet I got shot as a forest's doe
Bleeding on the ground, gasping
With nowhere to go
The hunter killed me and ate me
Now I'm Joe Rogan's shit
Please don't hate me
But I am The Prophet
Privately landing in Moffett
You thought I'd say his name?
Well I will—It is Muhammad
Without relation to Islamists

I am the gears that make the clocks tick
I'm blasphemy, hypocrisy, and the first stone cast
When she was accomplice to murder,
I was P. Diddy's loyal-scared lass;
I was Jennifer Lopez's ass.

I am now Jupiter
Yet Neptune escapes me
I am Prometheus
Yet Zeus evades me
I'm even the flame I gave
I'm a drunk girl at a rave
I am Mesopotamia
I'm cradle to grave
I am the fourteenth Louis
And I built Versailles
I am the Sultan of Brunei

And his brother Jeffrey
Jet-setting with state's full coffers
And I'm the women he takes on the plane
Only after Prince Salman ran a train
I saw it, felt it all, for
I am he,
And those girls on which R. Kelly peed
And I am Jeffrey
I am Mother,
Nipple and baby
I'm the only one who can save me
Though whispers yell, "He's crazy!"
I am thee, all of ye,
So I ascribe myself hazy
You already paid me

For I am the rain that washes away
Your childhood tears
I am the pain that recedes from the years

I'm Little Boy and Fat Man
I am autodidactic
I'm the Blitzkrieg tactic
I am the Navajo
For I broke the code,
I am Leonardo, the revenant,
And DiCaprio's biggest boat

I am the world
I am all else
I am the Big Bang's belch
I'm a loner

I am the crowd

I was the bruises on Rihanna
I am Diana; I'm The Immaculate Madonna
I'm also Madonna and Disney's Jasmine
Bare in sauna
I am every Princess, yet
Also Leopold
With his rubber in foreign land
Like Ford in Fordland:
Him too.
I am Henry and
His peasants,
And ev'ry story ever told.
I am Midas' gold
And Homer's own odyssey—
That Poet was only old.
But I am a god ageless.
I am his foretelling sages.

But for all that I am
For all the civil wholes I tore
I can't make them care any more
About me—those girls in all
Will care less in time's strife
But I can make them
Care more for their life

For I am the killer venom
And suburban Eminem
Or the bug in his trailer park bed

I am every tear ever shed.

I am the ink of Voltaire's pen
I am Trudeau, I am Rousseau
I am everything Hobbesian
I am Locke and Lockett,
The Eternal Recurrence
Noble stoic linear pocket
The light Caravaggio depicted
Was I obscured
As were Plato's cave's Shackled Convicted
The shadows on the wall were also I
And I them as well for all of time
And when the enlightened one returned
I was him too
And the sun he saw from sky blue
I am the reaper, I am life's Victor
I am Frankenstein and his monster
I am Murderer's Row
And the Yankees' 1927 roster
I am a monster;
Maniac;
Insomniac
Every pin-striped mobster
And that gentleman
Who invented RICO
And every imposter
And those who stayed loyal
You get the ideal
I'm poor and royal
I'm a righteous sinner
With nowhere to go

With the time of forever
Still too short for me
'Tis for all ye
Gather here near manic spree;
Hear ye! Hear ye!
I am a god

I used to be the boy that felt cared for
That's the only thing I'm not anymore
But forget about the boy
Forget about the man
Forget about those stretched with holes in hand
I am the ones who said they'd never leave
And the one abandoned eventually
I am the reaper and live flesh
I am what doesn't kill you
And the pain that makes you odd
I've been left too many times
Stranded alone and abroad
By another broad
But I assure you;
I am them too.

Behold! The man who never was
The child born ever-lost
Who alone bears his cross
At least it's simpler this way
I am he who achieves his goal:
His name was Sid the Kid
I am flatulence, laughter
I am the victims of Assad
I am the gaseous night

I am Cassius' fight
Mohamed Salah
And Muhammad's Allah
Hiding in plain sight wordplay
And the girls who would never stay
I am the people and the quivering force
Though death is finality's resource

For those who think I'm not
Have already proven my cause
I am the narrow and the broad
And now I am a god

The dry heath endless
And Nikola's breathless ledger
Of notes and scripture relentless
I'm both birds of one feather
And a pigeon; that pigeon with
Nikola's white smidgeon.
Space bound musk's mantis
Do you understand this?

By now there is no "you"
Just a mere reflection in view
And the oversight of the Overman
Yet I am one of one, always two
Only *my* dreams come true.
I am the baby who cried
The same one that, in time, died
I am suicide
Yet always alive

The dirt and gravel gray-brown scars
I live among Neptune and the stars
Yet the sea's bottom is brighter than Mars
The darkness is my light
As I am a loyal wife
And a faithless groom
I am the spacious room
Only defined—like Lao Tzu's cup—
By its empty void
Measured by what is not there
I am nothing, for
At least filth takes up space
I am the only one with no face
Chanel's favorite political party
High fashion from Paris
And Hilton's favorite party
Where coco runs down its own slope
I am that great white hope
That dilated eye screaming
That crimson from pink nose
That treadmill that heathens like
And hedonists fucking for one night
And the drink that cures the pain
And the syringe that ends it
I am Pain
I am the rain and the river delta
I am the great black gap
That leap of faith
And faith rewarded
After bloody socks trek toward crowns
Basquiat from above frowns
But since I am him

I smile from The Down
I am the bounds and the beyond
Afraid of nothing
And the trigger, the finger, the man
The hairpin
The grenade
The last war
The first serenade
The bed where Washington laid
Finally, I am afraid—
The angst of Kierkegaard
The merchant of death
Red barons in the sky
A beating heart with no valentine
Packing lips of cyanide

I am the assassin's grin
Every saint's sin
The nature of whims

Although my story is time-old
I still wonder:
Why is Winter cold?

I suffer the most plight

I already told you
That I am the night
I am a god

And I love these words with a passion
This page as my final bastion

I seek solace no longer
Body withers; every word stronger

I am the reason for Noah's existence
Flooding pages intrepid
I am pacifist insistence
I am ivory resistance

I am a god

God, I am a god—
Greater than all below you
Just under you
Only inferior to Your Majesty

Lord, forgive me, for I am above
All your creations
And if hierarchy be so, then intimation.
Annihilate all those below

I am a god.

Forgive me, Lord. Please.
"I just do this publicly."
I am a god.

I
 Am

A god.

Today I Tried To Cry

Today I tried to cry
I tried to cry today
But my eyes stayed dry
Though the dark ne'er rid itself

I looked up to dreary night
And shivered
O, oppressed stars withered
From moon they sipped;
My eye twitched

I blinked and breathed
Frigid wind chilled bones
Brittle and broken roads
I looked ahead alone
With dry eyes
Atop swollen bags and
Weary feet under knees
Sharp and sore
But one step at a time
My faith grows
I stay high in the lows
But dotted stars do show
Constellations connected
Night dims any light, though
A tragedy of plights rejected

Though the night be protein's starch
And the wind nigh unjustly harsh
My every step a stride

Every walk a march
Every mountain high a mile
Every hill weathers my smile
Every mountain a mile
But a tear is nigh
In the dreary sand do
My eyes drown in dry
As caves no longer speak
And the time fades as
Black night rears its head
Shimmering lights fade to ash
From overhead

But when all is dim
I don't worry

Today I tried to cry

Today I tried to cry
Though my eyes stayed dry
My feet kept moving—
They've never failed me.
Past desert and purple sea
Though cold road cracked, see
I didn't dare to flee
I beckon to come and get me.
For though fallen tears
Of downtrodden years
You cannot be me.
Smear me. Try and see :)
Little debutants look on and seethe.

Bipolar Biopics

It's cold it's cold it's cold
It's cold it's cold
Chilling spine tingles
Shrilling scream
Penetrating screech
Piercing 'ah'
AAAHHHHHHHHHHHHHHHHHHHH
Still silent
Ice from sharpest stream
All drops nightmarish dream
That's what it is, sincerely
But, Mother, it's been cold dearly
Even in LA
Even in Summer's stay
Blank gray skies lined with fortune so
Eagles from nest so far to go
Birds of a feather have no more than
One wing to show
So kill it
And kill them both
Kill them all
Their little bloody heads
Sprayed paintings tall
Basquiat's, Picasso's,
Monet's, Caravaggio's—
Figures dead
My muses red
For such art, effusive
Tasty meat along the way
Then what is left is bone

The road will crush and grind
In gravel-loud tones
Always eagles the same
Flying high until
That silver pellet strikes pink gold
The bird falls into silver snow
Its eyes dim and lose their glow

But traipse onward
For the gunshots are loud
And the leopards prowl light
On their toes in sun bright
Lurking eyes shine brighter in death
The stink of bipeds fill the air
Gunpowder and ash-gray do fare

But damn it.
Damn it all.
How do I apologize?
Or even should I?
World teeming with viola
Tions
Of all sorts
Vio
Lations
But what's transgression to a set of steely eye?
Now, the eagle's dead and the snow grows
Now, the nest dies and the soul's growth slows
Now, you can't dream of one thing but death,
For that is life.
Ah ha!
Good luck with the rest.

For life's but awaiting death.
Forget a mating plea's breath
For life is awaiting death
And
Cold
Winter
Abides
By
Your bones
And soaks
Your sleeves
And binds
Your fingers blue;
Murdered eagles make
For dead-eyed singers:
Eagles red-dyed harbingers
Speak as they die, this idea:
Rivers always reach the sea.

Rivers always reach the sea.

But wander.
And keep so
Stepping strides
In proud rhythm
In tone strident
Coriander mist
Starflower sun fruit tropics
Take a trip
To the bipolar biopics
Snow covers warm beaches
No breeze or cold in arctic reaches

Sunny nights make for dark shirt's bleaches
A bipolar biopic
And you're watching the feature

A person feeling the worst
Makes for great entertainment
Ornery chimps trapped captive
Idiots in passivity
Bipolar morons retarded
Bipolar morons retarded
Who can't see the way

Unless,
Maybe,
They see
Every way
The world can feel
And are only told
They are crazy
Based on studies old.
Maybe those bipolar invalids
Carry news that must get through and
Carry tales of great prophecy

Crazy people should be alone
Bipolar neurotics should be away
Cast them out
Of society's way.
And yet,
Those invalids build new ways;
Isaac Newton had a thought.
Mahler wrote quite a lot.

Hemingway with pain wrought.
Coppola showed new ways of screen.
Poe told tales never seen.
Do you ascertain Van Gogh's picture?
Have you drank Virginia's tincture?

Thank those crazy ones
Those bipolar and the neurotic
Those unable to be robotic
And children of same tongue and brain
Broken minds bear beauty from pain

You know it's true.
It could even be you, for
I am He;
I am She;
Bipolar words
Two poles of same sphere
Their wide-eyed terms
And careless actions
Wild minds
Can be tamed certainly
Those with two minds
Unstable, moronic, aggressive,
Depressive ones,
Though the enraged
Beget instability
Their words
Cast certainty

Fortuna

Fortuna
Oh, Fortuna!
Please be mine.
I take chances on your love,
Sweet kiss; gold mine;
I rely on you all the time.

Loved by all
Sultry, smooth, and tall
She is lusted over
Drooled over
Dream's subject for endless fools,
Subject of delight on many moons,
Her skin is tight,
Her pillow lips supple,
Her legs thick up high and long in the small;
She's gorgeous past measure
And supreme Goddess above all.

Supple skin rolls like hills
Over bony hips that stick
Out like a model's model,
Sweet and purely sonsy
Body shaped like a coke bottle;
Surely
Gold is an insult to her.
The sun pales in her glow.
Sweet, delicious Fortuna,
We praise all that you know.
Or what you choose

Or what your rosy pit contains
For your crevices are flowers
And your sweat is luminous;
Fortuna, I love you.
I need you.
I adore you, Goddess of Luck,
For the winds to blow my way
Or the proper girl to stay
Or that wistful candle to light the way.

They all want you, Fortuna.
They all need you, my beautiful Goddess.
Though they all pray to you
In feasting and toast,
I assure thee, My Love;
My rose-lipped host—
I need you most.

Fortuna (Epilogue)

"And so we obviously can't sell this. Let's keep it off our shelves."

"Uhm."

"Mm-hmm."

"Absolutely. He's not part of the... well, you know. I'm glad we all agree."

"Uhm... to a degree."

"What do you mean? I thought we're aligned in what we see."

"Well, I know it's edgy, but, hear me clearly: I think we may better be able to control Oliveri if we distribute his vulgar drivel."

"What do you mean? How would that be civil?"

"Because we could destroy his reputation; he's evil."

"I'm listening...."

"But hold on, this could be his literary christening!"

"Just let him speak! His idea could be riveting."

"But he objectified women! But he turned a goddess into a sex symbol! I think that's sickening."

"Okay, he may be all those things... but there's a market for this itching. And then, as soon as he sees success mainstream, we turn the tabloids against him and crush his dream."

"Hmm."

"Mm-hmm."

"So you're saying—just to be clear—we could publish his filth and get paid, then destroy his career that we made?"

"Hmm.... Give him light to darken his shade?"

"That's exactly what I say."

"But what if he shines too bright before we take his pay?"

"There is not a chance his work sees such a day."

"I concur. He could never be a mainstay."

"Yes—right you may be. So when he reaches his height, we kneecap his might?"

"*But,* say he—"

"Thinking nonsensically. He's like a baby—like twenty-something. He doesn't know how we run things."

"Precisely my point. We take his royalties and he is then controlled opposition for coin. At worst, he'll even join...."

"No. we can't make him part of us. He's an outsider... a useful fool; a clown—he needs tomatoes thrown; he needs to frown."

"Yes, correct. But he will never see an audience past what we can give him. We will simply grant small passage for short time and take all his money for his mind."

"I like it."

"As long as we own his copyright and licensing, it could be enticing."

"Yes, then we can control what he says. His diction; his prose."

"I'm willing to see how this goes."

"Agreed. I like the vision you've proffered."

"Then let's make Nick Oliveri an offer."

A Perfect Moonlight's Subject

Soft night
Scars delight
A Burgundy flight

But soft eyes
Gleam not
For naught

And lights way there
Kindle things here

And if shadows
Are from flame
Maybe not things
I feel from pain

So those
Soft eyes
Under blanket of night
Need not speak
Of any one thing.
Because they don't speak;
They sing.
They take.
But without music
Life is a mistake.

The Greatest Mediocre Story

"They say the greatest stories have already been told, but who the hell are they?"

Who the hell are they? Who the hell are you?

"Who am I? I'm the one that said the quote. And now I'm being quoted by you."

By whom?

"By you!"

Like me, me?

"Yes, you!"

How do you know who I am?

"You're the one who's writing me!"

Well, maybe so, but I'm not writing you to know me. This is my page, you know. This is my domain; my sanctity.

"Yes you are, you're doing it right now. I'm going to 'cross my arms and huff' now, aren't I?"

Well, it looks like you already did. Haha.
"Did you just write 'Haha' As if this is a text? How lazy are you? Poetry is not an SMS."

Lazy enough to not even finish this sen—

Reader, the monster in your head—I am He. I am She. I am They. I am It.

Do not, for the sake of yourself, try and dim me or quell me or kill me. What a fruitless pursuit that would be. I am the breeze laced in your brightest horizon. I am the mud and the silt of all of your toxic swamps. Do not sanitize your festered breaches.
Learn to get dirty succumbing to the leeches.
The eels and the worms like screeches.
Hear the screeches. Supple dermis separated.
Yell. No one can hear you.

The Conjurer is working his magic, and it's costing him his life. But freeing the world is worth a prison's strife.

What if chaos was coordinated? What if we could listen to the monsters in our mind? What if we were more of the monster than we may be kind?

"Packs work together effectively to isolate a herd animal, sometimes one that is ill or infirm, and pursue it to the death. The victors often squabble over the spoils, either among themselves or with other powerful animals like lions."
-National Geographic

I make art with words.

I reference others,
Past lovers burn;
They had their turn.

"If you hear a voice within you say, 'you cannot paint,' then by all means paint, and that voice will be silenced."
-Vincent Van Gogh

There is No tiTlethere is no title thereThere is notirr;e
There Is No Title Here

There is no
Title there.
And me? I fit quite nowhere.
I was too poor for those rich,
Yet held disdain for plebeians.
I was like a strong oak tree—firm, healthy, resolute—
planted on a tropical beach.

I was completely and utterly out of control. I was
bereft. I was lost. I was caught in the subterfuge
of an indifferent tsunami.

She was all I had.
She made me healthy.
Then I lost her.

There is No tiTlethere is no title thereThere is notirr;e
There Is No Title Here
(Epilogue)

It's simply not true.
I never lost a one.
I've never tripped none.
The world moves
Yet I
Stay still

It's a lie; that poem was simply art to entertain
Nothing real from which to maintain.

It's all a sham.
I've never lost anyone.

I was never healthier only because

Someone

Was with me
To alongside atone
For my sins and vice.
Don't ask me for advice.

I can do it alone.

I can do it alone.

"You think he's still thinking about you?"

"Of course he is."

"I love your hair dyed. The pink looks nice."

"It's because I'm a new person to entice. You know I'm what the boys like."

"Oh, I love it and love you so much!"

"I have no love for even a perfect man such."

"Oh... so he was perfect?"

"Oh, no, far from of it."

"Okay, but you still got that big booty!"

"Okay, I'll be fine."

"What's your last name without a man, Hanna?"

"Almuti...."

"Big booty Almuti! And you don't need a man!"

"Yeah, you're right. And I know who I am."

Hear The Echoes Of The Nether

Jagged needle teeth
Dripping in malice
Is what I see
When I close my eyes

So I pry them open
From gruesome demise

A black hole swirls beneath
Its malevolence unmatched
It heartily laughs
At me
Daring me to jump
Beckoning me
To be swallowed
Wholly and fully
Into shadow's descent

The leatherbound book of old soothes me
Hewn from the great stone of centuries
Forged and written by the masters of old
Trampled and lost; tarnished gold

Live your own stories. Tell your own stories. Form
your own images and then believe them. Go live.
Live a true story worth telling. You have my blessing.
Your stories live in your head and then forever if you
like.

For your own journey is all you have.

Like sand through your fingers, everything else lies.
Like wind clear passing by, all else is demise.
There is chaos within you that belies truth;
Do not turn from it. Do not run from
Your own known.

You've been lied to. Your life does not consist of
The stories you find. For too long you've stared
And ignored your mind. For too long
You watched shadows that have diverted your eyes
From the real picture; you have worshipped
The pithy pyre and have rejected the sun!

There is beauty all around you, among you
And within you. Look around!
Show me a captive listener and
I will show you a lover of decay!
You fear the spear and therefore your greatest
Triumph is dabbling in bleak nothingness.
Merchants of dust. Ashes to rust. Even iron is such.
You are no more resolute than iron bone. You wait
Patiently
For a gravestone.

This is a dangerous book;
A foreboding collection
Of prohibitive perception.
It is a paradigm-shifter
Of grotesque conception.
It is a dangerous book
Hark! 'Tis a dangerous book
Ban it. Burn it thus.

For its words are cancerous.
Rid the world of its toxicity.
Toss it.
Cancel it.

Its dangerous truths are laced in malevolence.
Nothing lies underneath the diction of this work
other than chaos and the untamable, unwilling
beast, and He prefers *not* to be seen.

It gives me no hope and quells what I thought were
inner visions of a fairer future.

WARNING: EXTREME CONTENT

Always quick to know
Always slow to forget
That little one with blue eyes
With the bangs
The one with the hips
Lots there in little frame
Lips full of lies
Winning fake game
Smile so sweet
Embrace me
But she sold me
For pennies.

Now I live literary
In third person
Sickly

I miss you and your full pink lips. I miss my
{censored} along your {censored} {censored},
Gently... {censored} slowly, written for vulgar lowly.
Conflict always. You were my fleshy colosseum.

Great art needs not some mausoleum.
Great art can be as practical as the breaths
And the tired steps of everyday life.

There is simply no other medium that can suck you
up and spit you out quite like the written word. It is
not only the greatest, but also the rawest and
mightiest of forms, characterized both by the air of
the heights and the crud of the varmint low silt,
barons heir apparently in service to forever poems.
Lo.

Sometimes, my paranoia creeps
That words will go obsolete.
Then I remember that
Words are all we have, all we've ever had.

Prometheus gave us flame in vortex.
Words are but humanity's torches.
The future lies within my cortex.

I care not if I am a sage.
Wisdom be damned.
I have only this age—
All I have tonight is this page.

Dedication Part 2

Dedication
To prime life's simple way
To master what it's given me
Has beckoned more than a day or three
Lonely hours turned to cold
Turned to pages turned
To burned manuscripts
To a king, a fool, a beggar
Then a revelation's script

To prime life's simple way
I've had to master simply
What it's given me
And taken the time
To 'ah ooh aah' in cadence
In rhyme
Then refine
And refine again and
Refine again,
For life's resistance
Is met feebly with pen:
The heaviest tool my hands could lend.
And yet, be it beggar, king, hermit,
I present to you
A lone figure's sermon:

Standing in black or colors or the absence of others
I'm crass and innocent and still dilettantish
New and green, wearing all the things
Now internal rhyme schemes have

A belonging sense for,
End rhyme beckons more
And the poems keep coming
The
More
The
Earth's
Dirt
Spits and shines humming
I despise couples loving,
Applauding desperate things
Broken people
But you might not have the time to read this.

I said,
"But you might not have the time to read this!"

But it's silly when you think it;
This is just the dedication.
And only Lil Wayne comes to mind
Upon further meditation.
Like at three AM alone,
Typing my Devastation.
It's art. Its art amazes.
So that's my dedication;
You need this book
To witness dedication, its... it's unwavering
In its exploration
Every detail from middle to
Beginning
Writes its own ending
In a way you never could.

Or should I be humbler for
Those who stood for
My rights when I simply
Had none?

So this book may be an answer
to page endings
Or life's empty chapters or
Challenges beckoning more
From your spirit's sacrificial door
Eternally you read a book
That sets you from a safe moor
Whose words you can't take back,
And can't unlearn for,
You'll never forget, whore.

This is my world.
So let the pages keep spinning.
It gets dirty, but I won't warn—
You are but a plaything.

This playwright is amazing!
The actors are all puppets.
The props are but passing things.
The vocalists can only sing.
Yet, you are but a plaything.

It is the playwright's world, now.
Set the stage for urbanscapes
Or endless cattle grazing.
While my blind conductor stands waving
I grin in smiling shadow, I look on toward

The blank audience I assuage.
But you?
You are but a plaything.

Red claws writhing against a million of the same
You are a nematode feeding off the filth of past
There is no more blood to be had
Despite all of that to last.

Dedicated to me and everything
What I do is perfectly
Fallible.

And I also take missteps alone.
I also stumble and my thin
Skin gets cut by foam.
It's just that my cuts
Are bold pieces of art and such.
My words are not mirrors;
You may also not be much.

INTERLUDE ONE

I was delivered unto a place where the only color was gray, and my only birthright was the dirt beneath my back. I was swaddled in used rags, abandoned in a trench where disease was the rule, not the exception. They don't have a word for "sadness" where I'm from; it's just called "life."

Sickness, crime, addiction,
Bite of the snake's strike—
The sting of scorpion:
This is my origin.

Purple Heart

Funny and kind
Not kind enough
Often goes high
Not high enough
Cigar smoker
Too much of a loner
He's still in school
And not one for rules
Too short
Too many warts
To hide
Reckless mind
Feckless drive
Too much, too little
Too steadfast
Or too fickle
Never in the middle
Tears and smiles
Masks and miles
At record speed
Never takes heed
Sacrifices made
For love to grave
Only works
Always hurts
Plays with words
Subject to burns
Gives too much
Until giving is dumb

Hurt too much
Until feeling is numb
To sky
Asks why
Gets high
Feels nigh
And every
Single time
Singles out
Every rhyme
Bitter thoughts
Sour lime
Single mind
Single line
Mending nill
While never still
If you've gotten this far,
Know that it's his heart
That's a wish of Hell's
It has always ticked
For someone else
Most sensitive ear
Has never heard bells
Oceans apart
Broken shells
One wish
Heart breaks
One stitch
Couldn't fix
Gashes hit

He's Ambition's greatest gift.
He is Love's foremost fit—
Lovesick
He's never fit
Regret
Begets loss
Always lost
Fell off
Short-changed
Heart maimed
Ripped off
Victim of sin
One surprising win
Looked in the broken glass
Saw the destroyer of him
Then the lights dimmed
With dilated eyes
She betrayed him
Held the glass
to his chin
It pervaded skin
Shards within
Blood spilled
Red and blue
Tasted tart
Purple Heart

Gray sun
Gray road
Crashed and burned
Eyes closed

Shocked
No power node
Left behind
Never home
Felt alone
But for this tome
Seven homes
He was owed
But that's his mind's main crime:
He thought life would be sweet
Then tasted sour lime
Gray road tar
Love is war
Red and blue blood
Purple Heart

Red and blue blood
Purple Heart

A Village Isn't Civil

When the moment seems endless
Nigh matters if dawn approaches
Traipsing by barren steppes
Begets delirious regret.

But why turn back
When you know the price of the path?
If relentless brown dunes are all you see,
Then why not face uncertainty?
For if behind you lay
Festering corpses, birds of dismay,
Derision, starving trees, and mockery,
Then why delay
On continuing on
And taking that next step?
It could be toward freedom;
It could be toward death.
Yet if your only options are forward or past
Don't hold sacred that which can't last.
Head in tall regard and light strides—
Don't turn back.
You are all too good,
Though vulgar and crude.

Now you're being pursued;
Now there is one option true.
Step forward. Walk on. Go live—
The plains seem barren and endless
And the winter's bite cuts in sharp,
And the townspeople will mock you

Until they try to kill you.
Head held high—
Either way you'll die
So, you may as well try.

Move forward, though chances be nigh
Past thin and thicket, through lances and spite.
For beyond the flames of evermore
Lay a cleansed and virgin canvas—
It beckons you forth
So, run to it.
You regardless will be mocked and pursued
So wander onwards toward your pursuit.
Now is the time.
Opened mind, take a breath
And a stride.
You may at first be lonely
Then over time,
Community;
Many you will unite.
Then a dove flies your way
As the trees don't seem so barren
And the breeze clears the sky
Open arms, gushing charm,
Her deep brown eyes keep you warm.

Then the dove flies away
As you can't keep it caged

The village diatribal
And alone again
You gaze toward miles

You have no choice.
No one beckons for your company
And you are pursued again;
Only for the lonely
The devil disguises as a friend.
But if demons flank
And wolves grow hungrier
And the howling winds do beget
The coming ages
As time ensures,
There are no ageless faces.

Onward.
Walk onward!
Bore your hole heavenly
Irreverent sanctity
Walk onward!
Past chill rain and damp air
The scent of storm and despair
Walk onward.

Toward furious seas
'Yond jagged trail lies destiny
Smile, though cut feet get weary.
Smile, though you walk your path alone.
Smile, though your face hangs heavy.
Laugh, though you have no home.
Carry onwards—
Go! Live fully.
Stare at the sun and face the bully.
Now, live more fully!
Your time has come

And it's always been now.
Always too late;
Urgency awaits.
Green ponds and ecstasy
Over more hills at epic speed

And the best part:
Through all the pain and derision
You'll never find it. Ha!
For "it" is not a thing.
It's a figment, a wish; life's cyst.

Though you met much brokenness
You found reason to exist.

Congratulations.
You persist.

Your own path was the gift.

I Pray For You

I pray you find peace.
You can pray for me,
Or pray for the weak.
For peace is not what I seek.
Pray that my clouds turn bleak.
Pray I walk through the pit of danger.
Pray that I can't control my anger.
Pray I fall down it all.
Pray dearly on my downfall.
Or you can pray for the weak,
Or the meek,
Or you can pray for me,
But it is not peace I seek.

Epstein Did Not Kill Himself

I can't conceive a next step.
For how could life progress
If there are future regrets?

I cannot be loved, so don't love me.
It is my fault, so don't trust me.
Another lost one, unlovable—
Too foolish, vulnerable
Manipulate and hate me
Rape me
Hold the knife behind your back
And pull the shiny silver out
And threaten and hold me down
And plunder the well of my mind
And loot my spotted soul for riches;
I am endless wealth for you bitches.

I am a black woman, so, please
Tell me what I should believe in.
Dictate to me, you Educated Ivory,
As I need coddling.
Proffer me what to think and believe;
I will submit and never grieve—
Unless I am told so.
For, I apologize to
You Mighty Towered-Secluded
For all my slander
And ire misguided—
We are far too divided.
And I need to assimilate;

We need to stop the hate.
I identify with a
Society homogenized;
We are all perfectly alike!
We are all the same!
Is it not a beautiful age
That we are on the same page
And we all agree,
As one proud country,
That Epstein did not kill himself?
Allegedly.

Jeffrey Epstein
Did not kill himself.

Forces were at work;
The Force is female.

I Am Still A God

I fail only to purport false truths.
For by moon blue when I do,
The light still seems to spill truth.
From my rapid lips drip acidic malice congealed,
Yet from my pen, open scene of horizon unsealed;
This arctic arena I face myself in this point alone.

Now I see through those blind
Making material those euthanized
And those truly too slew-footed
To nurture who and why.
These questions in my head, they lie,
As I've made mine
And laid out for all time
To create these creatures
From demise
Again.
And yet again,
My heated pen blazes characters of charcoal lava
Melting away the forever-frost, chilled no longer,
I speak to lone page on my own;
There is no place or state quite like this home.
Here, may my reach always be limitless,
Operatic prayer beyond conception of edges.
I can thaw the never-melting ice as I please.

These creatures lurking in your head
Are now empty sheets in your bed.

A ripened orange, a wooden door, a mystery;

Fake Diasporas selfishly forsake history
Constantly propagating until endless story
Comes to an end
Impending.

And I did all this with a pen.
To you who hears this
And properly sees it,
For what may not be where
Or what never was
Is now there for all time.
If what is in your mind
And what's contained in eye
Is within fine neural confines,
Then I just changed your mind.

What I say is the truth.
What you heard has only been
Machinations of my pen.

The Breadbasket

Loose limbs float without stitches
Down red rivers, collapsed bridges
Mother! Mother: barren womb
Empty kitchen: rusting tomb

And brothers die
In crimson fratricide.

Blue bloods with yellow eyes—
Only in green do they abide.

But
Death has no color.

Once a port city,
Proud, my namesake and muse
Only sees in shades of gray.
Brothers, fathers, the Mother abused.
As the loose limbs discolor
Othered by the twos
The color-blind with yellow eyes
Are the only left amused.

Atop a lake of black gold
The breadbasket soon left
Sacred peace of proud protest....

I bear it; I feel it and wear it.
No tear too little; no cry too much
But in bearing it, I feel it's not enough.

Iron lines,
Flags and signs,
Fratricide,
None too wise;
It's all fratricide.

But who am I?
I come from Her.
She was when and where I was incepted
And she cannot tell me when last
I will finally be rejected.

Because proud people—
Once sisters, cousins, brothers
Become one body—
The land: my dear Mother,
She fires at and stabs herself
In crackling night, dehumanized.
Now I understand: it's suicide.

The Breadbasket (Epilogue)

"Mmm. Although amateurish in diction at times, Oliveri provides an insightful look at the plight of the Palestinian people. Though his diagnosis seems humanistic and laced with empathy throughout, he provides no real prescription or answers as to the ills of war. It is a good poem, but a little whiny. He didn't set a high bar."

"Oh, that's not *my* interpretation so far."

"So, you assert the poem wasn't about war? Or Palestine war-torn?"

"No, no. It seems to hearken to his home in sort of personal tour."

"And what home may that be?"

"Well, his birthplace, maybe."

"Oh! Hence the name of it: "The Breadbasket" as a reference to the Holodomor, perhaps."

"Indeed. And concurrently, it seems to be conflict he vaguely maps."

"I believe I see the connection."

"That's my conclusion after closer inspection."

"How about that last line, referencing 'suicide?'"

"It could mean those fighting are of the same ethnic ilk."

"Well, *I* think his words are incisive silk."

"Maybe for some stanzas—I especially predilect the colors as symbols."

"Hmm. Maybe a couple double entendres skillful."

"It seems he weaves unlike words with ease, willful."

White Pills and Purple Sips

White pills and purple sips
Can't come sooner to my lips.

Ivory pill and burgundy sip
Cannot seep sooner unto skin.

When my kidneys fail;
Bright unicorns prevail.
If my kidneys fail
Unicorns prevail.

Grow wings.
Pegasus carry me.
Married to a lady
Who only abuses
And teases me
She takes all my means
And hacks at my knees
Stealing from me
Constantly.

Pegasus, carry me free!
Bright wings and white mane,
Take me to a brighter plane.

Pegasus carry me fre t the
Place where clona z, no,
The benzodiazepines
Truly affect me
And help me with sleep

Catry me from mislpelling
My mouth closed; yelling.
You scoff at my editing.
My Pegasus will come, I assure you;
With nacreous wing and pure virtue
To fly me up into planes nether,
Above clouds, sky, severing tether.

I assure you it's all purposeful.
Cold tremors pierce nature's doleful
Means of surviving just to kill.
The violence is why I need a pill.
Or maybe two, or more still—
To my lips, burgundy spill.
Wash it the world down.
Watch the pain drown.

Rid me, please, of all sense.
Excuse me for my insolence.

My Pegasus came, see
I will be carried free.

I Cannot See The Devil

I cannot see The Devil; She is see-through
I sin and lie and drive until gray and skip food
Gazing into clear obsidian, I ask in earnest:
"Is there a piece of me considered purest?
Can a wretched vessel like mine gaze above?
Can a boy finite and weary find infinite love?"

Glory and spreading my story: the sewer of the soul
Showed me rats that chew, showing me the way
Through as they take my only food.
Lions are always few, as they don't need venom
To kill or sewers to view a life
Paved by scorching roar, in face blue,
Until their throats become sore too.

Walk alone. Walk alone! And if you do
The dark will come to you
But even the smallest spark is stark against night's
View on you. And it's all on you.
Even if you can't walk, talk. If you're mute,
Continue
To do
What the few do
And you'll see
A new you that says "yes" to life.
But when scuttling and slithering sounds
Like the only truth, and the sewer's youth
Grow old only to grow anew,
Just know that when they take from you,
Their sickness grows too. And they'll continue to.

The devil may be see-through, but he hears—
Just like you—a roar to a tune more akin to
A spark, then turns to flame's infernal fuel,
Hotter than the Sun God's red fire blew.

Burn few.

But let them see your light as it abides
By night's view of you; fight dusk and rise anew
Like young daytime light's golden view.
One fire spreads to more than few
If it treads to gore more than two.
And when it eats stores, the flame lets its light
Spread to the dead and
Burn bread to eat more and kill another slew.
Its righteous anger burns crowded hangars, too;
It devours gore to eat more and heat you.

For all the nights that covered its view,
The desert that starved its light's brilliant hue
Is now its pleasure as it stews
Grains of sand melt in its furious Hell.
It eats stars and rings to Heaven.
The devil may be see-through,
But let him see you.
Take heed of war and peace, too,
As you burn too hot for Hell's pot
And nights now-blinded view.
You can't see The Devil
But he sees you.

The Devil Whispers Wind

It's kind of a solace sometimes; the night.
Cold abyss, daring me to jump—I might.
It's been just pain for a while but—then a light.
Let me tell you the story of my plight:

Stars and sky
Seemed so far
And time passed long
And hours dripped, dried, and stayed still
And it all felt like nothing,
The worst kind of nothing—
White walls surrounded the night.
I used to think I was something.
And that feelings were just one thing
And that everything
Meant what I wanted to mean.
But then meanings went unseen
Because I simply stopped looking.
Those forever hours when petals froze
And dried and dropped to my toes
While I stayed confined in stolid hours
Staring stupidly at dead flowers
Taken openly by nature's cold glower
"There is no more me," I said.
In chill of wind on my spine, a grin dour.
The wind whispered, "then you're already dead."

Shrugging: "I may as well be lifeless in bed."

"Then I'll take your heart and the contents of your
head."

"I guess so. What use are they now?
All that was green has turned to brown."

"That's right," the cold wind said, "you frown,
You cry. You once had a smile, and now
It's your time to die."

"Yeah." I agreed with the cold wind.
"Take me and my mind," I said. "Take my Walking
Feet and pumping blood and please
Rid me of my useless brain."

The wind grinned. It blew colder in certain black.
All I could muster were shivers underpinned.
The wind cackled, growing darker and dim.
"And think of all the pain you've had—
Your life for others has only brought chagrin."

And so I took the wind's advice;
It struck colder, harsher.
On my mind lay only vice.
All the past pain, the future trials of
The coming cold rain; the oncoming guile;
I would never feel a gain.
I missed so much and freed from my soul
Greedy dragons I should have slain
And many battles I abandoned in vain.
Cowardice and avarice were
My last friends to remain.

But as the night grew darker
And the shadows made opaque,
My lips cracked a wry smile
In the core of my last strength.
I whispered to that vicious night:
"Is this all you think I can take?"

The wind's tempest stumbled slower.
I felt old man Winter grew yet older—
Withering weak shoulders.
His voice thin and desperate,
Spewing spite and spit and hateful rain
The storm soaked my jacket, my body
Frozen from frigid stains.

I laughed and cried out. "Is that all you got?"

"But you've suffered so much.
Your tears are meaningless—they can barely
Feed the dirt on which your feet land!"

"And yet," I said, "here I stand...."

"And try as you may," the night rasped, "all
Will turn against you and you will
Only meet dismay. Cold rocks will kick you.
Your lovers won't stay.
After all, you're unlovable, and *that* they all say.
I know you're weary, weak and dismayed.
I know your eyes puff red and teary.
You would be so peaceful
If you gave me your brain—

You promised me today!"
A small path opened which I took.
There was light the more I looked.

"No, thank you, but I think I'll walk on.
I've come thus far on a broken path,
But it's mine to take alone.
You couldn't possibly make me cold enough
To freeze me to the bone.
You craved my soul and wrecked my home."

"So why then, boy, do you still stand?"

"You could never make it dark enough
To sullen the light as things got rough.
You desire my mind and body too,
But these I cannot give to you.
If this is your worst, then I know I can
Smile through storm and harsher winds.
You almost ate me alive, swindled
My heart from my hands.
But today I stand.
Today, I am not your man."

I walked on
Though my pack grew heavy
Yearning for warmth and easy steps
On tired path, mind shattered, I walked on
I walked on.

Sitting In The Cemetery

I sit with legs crossed
In a field most alive;
The most visible here thrive.
O, these souls with so many stories to tell!
I listen. I wait. I close my eyes. I drink it in.
Past our pithy plane lies
A world without sin.

The bright sun is harsh;
The morning is dark;
I see figures walking;
They have no shadow;
Stones atop dirt shallow.

Tobacco had to burn for me to see
A Cigar smoke reverie.
World of apparition's memories,
Smoke-filled field unseen
Of live bodies still smiling.
Beautiful nightmares
Make riveting tales.
Infinity pales;
I assure you of this!
Angelic of bright gales!
Death is not final—
The tale begins only
When you are
Destined.

I've been to the void and never got out

Hello, here I am now.
It's the alien, the boy interplanetary
Writing salient tomes in cantankery
Traipsing all through bright cemetery
Silent stones moan on high.
Granite gems ever etched which never lie
Will stand long after you are alive.
"In God We Trust."
"Rest In Peace."
Sentiments of granite will persist
Long after we exist.
For, when the walking become drifting dust
Unseen spaces shall be ruled thus:
Stones and souls walk forever
Infinite until never
As we walk and witness the dead
Who remind us of what lasts true
Forever instead.
As life is a mere gap,
Fear not your final inception:
Peaceful resuscitation.
O, springful age of youth
Forever persists.
Do not fret once you exist;
Smile, for your fruitless toil
Pales to ageless sentiment.
In ultimate beginning
You will represent
The victor with the spoils
As you live beneath soil.
Even the sun can't end
An ageless smile;

Stars pale;
Infinity shudders;
Great wealth lies once everything is given.

I have lived all lives; take it from me—
There is a thing greater than infinity.
Trust me.
Smile.
Grin wider than crescent.
Laugh louder than flame in tundra.
There is no need to resent—
All that awaits is pleasant.
Peace you cannot find. In truth
It finds you.

"External obstacles are internal blockages always. Everything that stands in your way is only what you contrived it to be. You are more powerful than you would ever like to be."
-Nick Oliveri

Customized Lenses

Customized lenses
For custom problems

Customized pain
Lusting eyes vain

Sacred smoke caresses
Custom tinted windows

Customized problems
Gluttonized retail
Fetish for metal
Covered in acetate
Crescent smile
Vicious white stakes
He stalks no prey
As he walks all day

Seeing the world
Through customized lens
Rapid means
Justify vicious ends
He sees the stars
Up sky. But
Looks down and sees sand.

No matter—
Those brushstrokes are his
Two lenses the same;
Forever like twins

Sharing same name.

Grays pervade nothing
For he sees something—
Pinks and blues
Want more than one thing

Answer the question:
What is his bastion?
Draped in silk:
Acetate's his passion.

No matter!
No matter—but
It all matters
To him.

Fake ghouls steal
And renew fears.
Yet acetate
Shields the tears.

Customized Lenses (Epilogue)

"I told you he likes to spend."

"Is that what this poem is about?"

"Without a doubt; I know him too well."

"I guess that makes sense… though it depends."

"Depends on what? I know he spends—I even offered money to invest and lend."

"Didn't he have more means to spend? Even if that time came to an end?"

"I guess so… but no. He squandered his payout, and now he is bereft."

"So he spent his money on glasses and… has little left?"

"Yes. That's when he went uneven."

"I guess he's stupid, then?"

"Not exactly. He just went crazy and is now impulsive."

"I understand. Want to exploit his mood explosive?"

"Always. They never end."

"I thought he was your friend?"

"He is my friend, but money is my end."

"Okay, then. I will worship it with you."

"In money's name, I pray for better view."

"And I pray for a fucking higher milieu."

"Don't push it."

"Okay. Sorry. Then I pray to the men with money.... Is that more like it?"

"Yes. Now touch it."

Winter Breaks

Buried
Winter break
Breaks him apart
Lines of salt
Line the walks
And the lines on
His face grow
Ever deeper

A cavern of lights
Grows dimmer
Ice building
Never simmered
In the cold
In the dark
Soul was sold
From the start
Pi ece s
Shards scattered
In his mind's eye
A world battered;
Don't cry.
Don't cry.
Tears only serve to flatter
The ones that scattered
All the shards
All over the cavern
Into bro ke n p ie ces .
Once earnest
Twice purposed

Thrice shattered
On purpose
Tried too many times
Now, trying is a kind
Of staying shattered
With a smile of sharp shards
Teeth like daggers
Ice is hard
P ie c e s
And then the hammer hits again
Dull smack against cracked skin
And then wind blows
Daggers like shards
Pieces sharp
Cut his heart
Cut his heart
Shivs feel nice
Blood makes art
Fade

The cold shiv feels nice now
My own blood looks beautiful
On the snow-white canvas
Paints pictures crimson
Released from prison
Cold shiv is warm and slight
Now I see the light
Fade

Oh, Nevermind

Nevermind
Or never mind
This meandering mind
Crumpled aside
Once strong has died
Taken for a ride
Lost without
Its pride
Two eyes
Both blind
To love
And suicide
To trust lies
Of the truest kind
She blushed
Then ruined mine
She rushed
To influence mine
My heart
Never truly mine
I searched
For bright love blind
But everywhere
I found two eyes
Sweet memories
Compartmentalized
Mortal fear
They've been hazed over
By my eyes dazed
With both hands tied

The lowest lows
The highest highs
Every time I blink
Mortified
I see her
Too alive
Death-defied
Now I'm crumpled
By the wayside
She had the truest eyes
And the sweetest lies
I knew not
What I had to climb
What was in front
Or what was behind
We crossed all
The thinnest lines
She made her way
Out of my life
Slowly and for her
My love had died

I'm on the moon now
The other side
The dark and cold
The stormy nights
Jump high
For the stars
Swarming god-bright
Yet efforts nigh
Slipped and fell
Couldn't fly

But through the lies
I've been clarified
Wish I could go
Back to blind
I shot for stars
They burned bright
They taught me
About the night
About the size
Of itself life
Immortalized
She is what
I'm sickened by
Rife with hives
Stricken by
An illness called
"Been deprived"
Of what I loved
Who I loved
Said goodbye
I turned and ran
Toward the sky
But I couldn't
Jump that high
Tripped and fell
Two black eyes
Seeing well
Immortal lies
Live forever
Inside my mind
They were all
One of a kind

Don't look
Too surprised
You've only been
Humanized
Before then
A tiny fly
But compound eyes
Could nigh see disguise
Nor could they cry
Heaven's goodbye
An angel sent
Never mind
She looked at me
Never mind
Blind eyes
Tastebuds
Sweetest lies
Tears flood
Who am I?
I'm who and why
She shot a glance
I bled and died
And put up for sale
They donated me
Not for measly fee
But for free

I've gained a savory taste for gray and brown dirt.
But you can't bury he who hails not from earth.

Sand Sits Or Stands

Sand stands
Apart from time.
It's swept and kicked
And has no mind.
It sits or stands
And shapes in hand
Engulfing world over,
Whether sea or land.
Its permanence
Fades
Always.
It has no trait
Nor needs a stanza break;
Hard and indifferent
Grains underneath
Our raw toes and feet
And legs wrapped in sin
Between torso
Forest gap to chin
And misty skin
And Hell itself:
A buffer
While the blue wind whispers its ills.
"It is so beautiful to suffer."
And the sand gets swept away
Always
I shudder at the wind's cold words:
"It is so beautiful to suffer."

Shattered Glass

White bullet
Rip through the red
Guts of the
Painful undead.
Committed, not addicted;
Conditioned, not afflicted;
The storm comes in,
Yet I've discipline.

There are those that can't.
And those that can't relate
To the ones who say they can't,
Or the ones that can't suppose
That victory is within a sweat and pant.
You should've never lied
Shattered window to my eyes
Peace in the shards of glass
Should've hidden the lies.
Saw the way she looked me in my eyes
Through the window to my eyes
But the white bullet shoots through
All the pain and lies
Erases the crimes
Severs the ties
Of knotted rope
Too strong for
Anything but
The white
Bullet

Gazing Toward Miles

When the moment seems endless
Nigh matters if dawn approaches
Traipsing by barren steppes
Arousing delirious regret.
But why turn back
When you know the price of the path?
If relentless dunes are all you see
Then, why not face uncertainty?
For if behind you lay
Festering corpses, birds of dismay,
Derision, starving trees, and mockery,
Then why delay
On continuing on
And taking that next step?
It could be toward freedom;
It could be toward death.
Yet if your only options are forward or past
Don't hold sacred that which cannot last.
Head high and light strides—
Don't turn back.

Now, you're being pursued;
Now, there is one option true.
Go forward. Go live—
Though, the plains seem barren and endless
And the winter's bite is harsh
And the townspeople will mock you
Until they try to kill you.
Head held high
Either way you'll die

So, you may as well try.

Move forward, though chances be nigh
Past thin and thicket, through lances and spite.
For beyond the flames of evermore
Lay a cleansed and virgin canvas—
It beckons you forth
So, run to it.
You regardless will be mocked and pursued
So wander onwards toward your pursuit.
Now is the time.
Opened mind, take a breath
And a stride.
You may at first be lonely
Then over time,
Community;
Many you will unite.
Then a dove flies your way
As the trees don't seem so barren
And the breeze clears the sky
Open arms, gushing charm,
Her deep brown eyes keep you warm.

Then the dove flies away
As you can't keep it caged

The village diatribal
And alone again
You gaze toward miles
You have no choice.
No one beckons for your company
And you are pursued again;

Only for the lonely
The devil disguises as a friend.
But if demons flank
And wolves grow hungrier
And the howling winds do beget
The coming ages
As time ensures
There are no ageless faces.

Onward.
Walk onward!

Toward stormy skies and furious seas
'Yond jagged trails belongs destiny
Smile, though cut feet get weary.
Smile, though you walk your path alone.
Smile, though your face hangs heavy.
Laugh, though you have no home.
Carry onwards—
Go! Live more fully.
Stare at the sun and face the bully.

Your time has come
And it's always been now;
Always too late;
Urgency awaits.
Green ponds and ecstasy
Over more hills at epic speed

And the best part:
Through all the pain and derision
You'll never find it. Ha!

For "it" is not a thing.
It's a figment, a wish, life's cyst.

Though you met much brokenness
You found reason to exist.

Your own path was the gift.

Get Stung

And then the door closed
Shut into darkness
The wheel of time
Has stopped for me
I have realized my chains
And some call me insane
But who is to blame
For who's good at the game?

Many will fall
And some will fail
But the mud-covered ones
Are sure to prevail
And so, my reader,
Get stung.
Get stung by the passages.
Get stung by the intimacy.
Feel the darkness and writhe senselessly.
Stick to your stories intrepid
Stay truly to your ideas stupid
Though reckless youth stay young forever
These words are black hewn in crimson
Stones cut but I could never die

Tell your story.
Just try.
It is only your experience,
Whatever that means.
It may be all you have.

Ashes

Tobacco burned
I look up
And ask why
Why live?
Why die?
With no response
I carried on
Then I saw her—
She was blond.

My cold face
Melted to smile,
And for a while,
I hummed.
But then she
Walked on by
I looked up
And asked why.
Tobacco burned

I'll never learn.

I light red draped in black,
This brown leaf is all I have.
Wilted tobacco burned.
I will never learn.

Ashes (Epilogue)

"So, do we know when he wrote any of these poems? Because that last one seemed like a kid wrote it."

"I sort of agree with that sentiment."

"I just feel like there are better poets we could've read."

"Maybe that one was just an impediment. Maybe he wrote that when he was an adolescent."

"Yeah, but I believe he was only twenty-four when this book was first published. And so I'd expect some to be rubbish."

"He was only twenty-four!? At his age, I was only a whore!"

They all cackled. Some women in the room took a sip of their drinks.

"Oh my *god*, aren't you just affirming what he thinks?"

"What do you insist?"

"Clearly, he's a misogynist."

"But we have to understand what he means!"

"I guess so… but for me, he's rather obscene."

"Oh, please, I've seen the smut you read!"

They all cackled in the room. One got up to pee.
Another took a nibble of duck confit. She gulped and
hoped no one would see.

"I just feel like he finds words to rhyme free. I think
it sacrifices poetic integrity."

"Yeah, I agree."

"In a way, absolutely."

The women all nodded with thee. A woman needed a
'we.' A woman couldn't be a 'me.'

"Wait! Aren't we playing into his typicality? After all,
we have doctorate degrees!"

"I'm sick as well of his misogyny."

"Yeah, me too. I'm sick of Nick Oliveri!"

"He could never capture the essence of women from
such a narrow perspective. It seems we chose the
wrong collection. He's just a boy who's been through
some rejection. *Boohoo*. So what? She left you. Guess
what, Nick? We'd all leave too."

The women in couches comfortable squeaked and
faked laughs. They sat in circle-path and threw my
book to the side, unwilling to read to the last.

It's a shame they didn't see it my way. I may be a
man, yet I bet they've been sad, too. I bet they've
cried alone, too. I feel as though you've had times
alone saying, "It's only me and you."

And then he or she or they leave, too.
I seem to suffer much like you.
In fact, our struggles are related—
Deep down, you want to do what lovers do.

I know it as well, see,
You may label me
All sorts of vagaries.
And yet the reality
Is that no label possibly
Sticks to Nick Oliveri

Sincerely,
Nick Oliveri

Verily,
Nick Oliveri

Epilogue over.

Big House, Small Pills

She's broken.
Bottles away from her past
Turned to sales
To try to buy the love she lacked
Big house
She takes small pills
Yellowing eyes
From a life of thrills
And as her kids have grown
The barren bottles have shown
But what about the house that's big?
Or the things she owns?
She sold things to take things.
Sold them to make them.
Disfigured by the machine's flame
Tears?
Mop them. Sweep them. Rake them.
Make them disappear under the giant
Floorboards of the big house.
After all,
The walls
Are big and tall
And can hide
The tears
That shook
The face of an angel.

INTERLUDE TWO

So far from home....
You walk with the devil
When you walk alone.

You may see Diddy and Bundy in Heaven.
OJ and Gacy if they are repentant,
But not those with bread unleavened.
That is the doctrine.

Though Jesus was {censored}.
He was the {censored} and {censored by Amazon}.
This third line completes my four-year triathlon.

And the darker s{censored} {censored}.
{censored} joined a welcoming cult.
Only the Irish can I insult.
Only the English can I skewer.
Despite {censored} without sewer.
While the bl{censored} {censored} nothing made
It is Slavs from which the term originates:
Slave.
SLAVE.

You {censored}.
{censored} you {censored} {censored}.
For these whimsical rules which I do not abide
I choose my freedom of speech while I am alive.

The Winds Of Thor

Winter Takes Another
But what does it matter?
Winter eyes down a
Squirrel's stash precious
Stashed with that which
Continues life
But the singing wings
with their lifeless
eyes, eye that which
continues life.
Swooping.
Cracking.
Feasting.
The plunder is sweet.
As the frost binges
on once sweet grass,
cold white covers
a squirrel's mane.
The feast escaped him.
But what does it matter?
What does it matter
that Winter claimed
another body?
Fringed by ice,
plugged by snow,
he sees white
and then eyes close.

A Face Too Frozen

A billion drops of rain
Yet no rivulets flee my eyes
Because I cannot feel the pain
Gray

But what of it? I paid to get numb. I paid for my
safety. I paid to wipe away the tears and get rid of
them forever. From what was earned went to
smoothing the edges.

I can't sit down; I can't stand it.

But it beats the tears; those rivulets from my eyes.
My pockets clanked with
A sack full of coins and change
Fresh-faced
Sun out
Walking toward the sky
But someone eyed me down
And told me to come by.
Fierce eyes, soft eyes,
And to this day, I thought a crime
She felt my arm
And stroked my face
And asked me for a dime
I continued on past her
Onwards and toward the north
Still heading for the sky
Now only one dime short

Sun-heated thin smile
With a pocket full of change
But I soon came upon
A booth square and tall
It blocked the street
A lady, to me, she called:
"You must pay the fee!"
I had a bunch, so I gave her a few
And still held that sunlit smile
With pocket-clanking change
But a slow wind soon crept
And the sun began to fade
Shivered to my bones
And struck with the magic of
Certain discomfort
I saw the coat I so needed
And walked into the store
The whole deal cost me much
And I even got charged more.
My pocket got lighter as
The jacket weighed me down
But the cold of the fading gold
Still froze my face.
I still tried to walk tall
In the face of it all
I was as only tough as
my pocket full of change.
The coins in my pocket
Faded as the crystal had—
blue to purple
Buds to snow
Raindrops became snowflakes

And although the coat
Kept me warm and near,
My face felt too frozen
To carry the tears.
Now I was cold and free;
No money.
No fear.
Life had taken me here.

Ode To {Censored}

I'm untethered
This is an ode to {censored}
I don't like it that much
And you can cancel me
Deplatform me
But I have my own mind
I'm down to pay the fee
Goal's not to get banned
But if it comes, then I'll smile
In the darkness
I'll be; waiting
And still saying
That even though I'm untethered
Can we not think about {censored}?
Of course, we can't. And I'm sorry for my rambling
just now. I deeply apologize. Sometimes my mind
becomes uncentered, and I end up thinking about
{censored}.
This conversation should not even be happening. I'm
sorry for even planting the seed in you.

The mind's grave has been entered
As we've broached the topic of {censored}.

They just care for
Your safety
And don't want you sad and blue
So I'll play by the rules
And I'll censor you.

Ode To {Censored} (Epilogue)

"And the report?"

"Yes sir. I have it right here—printed and copies for each of you."

"You already sent it beforehand. I want you to explain it firsthand."

"Oh, yes! I am ready to serve the nation."

"Get to it, then! I don't need some dissertation."

"Yes sir. I have his location and—"

"We just want his psyche explained and why his vocation."

"Well, firstly, he was diagnosed with—"

"We already know his medical history! Move on. This is for security."

"Uhm, yes."

"So what does he mean by the word, 'censored?'"

"It seems, Sir, that it's weapons to which he refers."

"Damnit! I knew he was dangerous. Go on."

"Well, it seems as though he has powerful means and is craftier than he seems."

"What do you mean?"

"He has a history…."

"Of what, specifically?"

"Of doing things, Sir, hysterically—I mean he has something that most don't have. I traced most of his experiences and calls. He always keeps people guessing."

"And so, what are the weapons?"

"That, Sir, by every metric is unclear. But we should detain him. No outlets should be informed."

"I need more."

"Well, it is known by those around him that he maintains certain characteristics."

"Do you have statistics?"

"Yes! Stats and anecdotal evidence. Here—read this."

"Hmm. And he has lived like this?"

"Yes sir; rather reckless."

"I'm not gonna' lie, I'm not sure where you got the weapons from."

"Yeah... he's eccentric, but what of his danger and disposition?"

"He is often changes position."

"That won't be hard to triangulate... in fact, we could see where he is right now."

"I asserted in the report that he won't be hard to track. That's not what this is about. Remember our models strongly suggest his influence which needs to be neutralized."

"I'm not seeing the connection for size."

"I concur—where is the direct link to his threat and anecdotal evidence you found that suggests probability around potential threats."

"Uhm, well, I was put on this profile for our program, as you know...."

"And you failed to go beyond the surface of his bottles and troublesome oddities."

"Yeah, is he a threat or not?"

"I maintain the models have chosen him for good reason."

"So? Do we target him or not?"

"To take him out wouldn't take a lot?"

"And what's the opportunity cost?"

"It's not great—we know where he is, and he is always lost."

"Personally, I don't see enough reason to take him."

"But, but, the models! They picked him out and I believe it's for proper purpose."

"Then what are the weapons? What is his threat besides being a fucking weirdo? Has he planned *anything*? Anything at all?"

"No plans so far, Sir, but I assure you, all of his habits and behaviors present potential problems for the public."

"But you know we need to link him to something."

"Did you read page forty-three?"

"Of the report? Yes. I did. And I understand the patterns, but it becomes costly and unjustifiable to make the case against him. This isn't even evidence—it's speculative!"

"Cancel his case, then. He is just a superlative."

Life Could Go On

Truly
No lie
It comes from a source,
A centrifuge of sorts.
All is dust
when one looks
at luminous glass.
Pertaining to few
It does not pertain to you.
Above your head
But out of your wallet
This is a travesty. Maybe there's a way around it,
though.

This poem is supposed to be about getting charged
as soon as you're born. Tolled. Taxed. Drained.
Decayed. Oppressed. Looted. The life is a loss always
until die, dying, death, coming quickly whether you
prefer.

Cracked skin and, eventually, bad hips. You, as in
everyone. But also you, as in you, personally.
Everything begins to fade as soon
as it comes into being's form.

But are we stars?
Meant only to be born and then shine?
If a star is only light
that only can we see,

Is demise the only option
Once light escapes sight?

I have a new word, though—I'll utter it now.
Maybe through birthing
Something other than ourselves
We can defy both the stars and the night.
Maybe we decay often but don't have to.
Maybe death is only for the weakened.
After all, we were created.

After all, we were created.

So what if I made,
As I fade and decay,
something whole—
A part of me that could never go?
Just think for a moment.
Use your own judgment for one second.
Is creation not the way to avoid decay?
Work and research throughout the day?
Maybe. But creation?
Creation could stay.
We see the light one day.
And before it leaves,
We pray.
And when I write,
I pray that
These words stay longer than a day.
You die, yet creation forever stays.

The Lamp

A lone lamp
Star without planets
In the night
Mist and echoes black
But it is bright
And it shines
For no one to see—
A beacon for nothing.
Is being alone
Definitely free?

It will fade one day.
One day it will fade.
And the only one
Who will know
Is the one who knows the shade.
But the mist is cooling
The light's constant fate.
No one it draws—
The lamp alone
Dies in its shade.
Needed by no one
Until it's too late.

Comatose

A single drop
A dolloping sound
Oceans abound;
It is calm.
But it is not peaceful.
Furious sounds of past;
Waves in my head;
The calm soon subsides.
And the storm sets in.
But comatose?
What happened to the calm?
I long for it again.
I pray for sun without end.
The dolloped drop in perfect peace
Made a murky-black splash.
And now the black rage
Of the indifferent seas—
Is all that I can possibly see
For miles
And miles unending.
The clouds shun stolid peace
Everywhere enemies.

Rip it all up. Sever all my ties. Rip this poem up.
Look me in my eyes.

The dark stays so long. It seems to set in
And never leave. Despicable sown seeds;
There is no fruit for those in need.
I write this currently

In the dark by window to nowhere vast.
I look for awaiting eyes and brains.
But I don't write to one. I just scrape this page.
Ferocity gained through blood
And I just hope it stains ye
Or a wall, I desperately plea!
For them to look and see.

Sometimes I can't simply stand it. Other times I
smile at myself.
I know you feel my pain.
I know you have the same hunger and cuts
As me.
But you keep your sleeves long
And your time spent short.
Glamor, glitz, shells of diamond smell
I look out and hope to find
What I'm looking for.

I want to run and fly and
Cast creations on the great rock.
My shadow puppets quiver
As they sing their final song.
I look out in the crowd again
And I see that she is gone.

Throwing Things

A flicker still burns
Flesh clean off
Soaking blood and staining clothes
With immolated rot—
Human skin.
Now it is smoking linen.
But what does it matter?
Hold a gaze.
But the void wins
The staring contest.
Every time.
And 'pain' is a stupid word
Because it doesn't matter.
And although my word is new,
It will fade once screens fade
And forever ice sets in.

I'm throwing things.

Tori
(Edit: this was not ██████████ ██████████.)

Assuaged into flame,
Deafened by the dull,
And deadened
By the doldrum stories venomous
She sank
But with a sharp edge
From the medical bed
She arose and struck down
The serpent.
And like a faithful seed,
She grew
From the flames
Stronger.
Now she can bend
Her body and mind
Not from the heat of the fire,
But through the power of her will.
Forever beautiful
And perpetually honest
To the nature
That loves her.
The yogi
The warrior
The sage and survivor
Not immune to venom,
But her goodness
Will survive her.

She had a certain shine;
All her browns:
Luxuriant
Mahogany.
Her tans: the sands
of the cleanest beach.
Dainty
Is the picture
Of her.
Strong
Are the fibers
Of her portrayal.
Echoing
Are the sounds
Of her sultry voice
In my head.
A Silk-laden sea
Colors her face
And hands
And sloping side.
From the lonely port
I began the voyage
Traversing that silk-laden sea.

Big-legged woman
Put a spell on me.

Tori

Embedded in smooth and
Endless java clean;
Two jewels—both hazel and pristine.
They span the distance
Between stars and space,
Universes within,
Bridging that moist gap
Splitting her wary heart
And a rapid mind
That ticks all-day
In an idle world;
She's bored.
With idle people,
She's bored.
She takes what she can
In a place that knows no better.
Pineapple fruit sweet
Her lips femme effete
And her rose mine painting-pink—
I never could get tired of her hop,
Her bounce defies polis
As she finds solace
In the dirty divine
And intuitive nature
Of the fluffy creatures,
The short and green,
The wagging tails, and
Cat-eyed clawed ones;
They dance to
The rhythm

Of her mind and body in tune
Alleviating
The indifferent pain
Of a cruel world's goodbye.

But that pain of theirs
Is also mine.

Black Widow

Black Widow
O, Black Widow
How you've woven your web

The tantalizing fibers of
your white silk are so soft and strong.

Your legs are needles
Which is alright
For what would silky thread be
If not for needles?
Your crimson hourglass is for the time we've spent.
And the capricious clock ticks—
But time does not exist
When I'm in your silk;
When your bite pinches
In your sharp kiss.
When I drink your lucid nectar
Your venom is sweet
As you prepare me to die.

I love you, Black Widow
Yet I am but a fly.

Little Pills

I used to play with pellets
Small, white, and round
Pull the trigger
Soft as air the sound

But those were kids' games
And welts were simple pain

Today I play with the same
Small white pellets
Supposed to keep me sane
But I chose madness
In a world so mundane
Now pellets cause more pain
No longer merely sting,
Now their deep cuts bring
No solace; clipped wings
Often too much,
Forever not enough
Roving and dreary such
That all is gray
And still mundane
Wandering in place
These white pellets
Give me grace

Unsure among zealots
Alone in crowded space
Little pills remind me
There is no happy place

So I wear all hues
Illusory blues
Reddened views:
"White kills black!"
We call that news—
I call it gray. These little pills
Dowse my flame, light my fuse
What a world or mind of shame.
I look into the mirror
For someone to blame
But only broken
Shards remain

These little pills
I talk to them
Weeping still
I pop them
Their creeping will
They make me talk more
Crying less; I want some more

Lit fuse has frozen,
I wander along now,
Meandering prose,
Or poetry walking,
Maybe a shard of glass knows,
Countless obsidian shanks.
From one canvas so clear
I try but I fear
That I can't change;

Lord knows I can't change.

Little pellets, white pills
Tiny devils, quite shrill
They do their work
And I stay still
Serenity is a pill

Serenity is a couple pills
Serenity dulls the thrill
Serendipity has no
Will.
Only pills.

Blind Gray Skies Of Fortune

And the bridges burn
As wind sears my face.

The rush of freedom
Constricts my lungs
And chokes the life from my eyes.

The smoke of the flame
Begins to faintly subside
As my chest goes alight.

More stoking.
Flame grins;
Poking.
Feeding a live flame
Hungrier than I
And greedier than I
And more ambitious than
A bright-eyed scion.
Then I walk on.

Then I walk on.

To the paths untraveled
Ready to get dropped
And unraveled
And flayed thin-sliced eyes.
I fight for Fortuna's
Blessing; "Please grant me
Ability to curl up away

From this world!"

But
There is a lonely thing
Which longs for fleeting feeling
Of long time away once feeling the sun
Tempering the bite of the crisp rain
With an unrelenting flame; hot means to
Yell, "I don't fear a soul or anyone!"
"I don't fear a soul or anyone!"

I don't fear a man.
No woman.
No they/ them.

I walk on thirsty.

And I walk on blurting
In crowds of blank eyes
Drinking to their demise
And hiding constant lies.
Constant lies.
Constant lies.
Constant deception.
Death does not grant
Any conception.

Towards the horizon unto paths untraveled,
Ready to get cut and burned, unraveled.

It is, to my chagrin, a travesty of all travesties.
But tragedy is more beautiful

As it burns brightly up close.
And from afar, a star.

These words come through the lens of
Choice as my insides alight
with opportune time for
Final flame of mortal fear.

And it was brought on.

The smoke quakes the musty air,
Obscuring broad shadow unfair.

Now my vision is clear.

Past smoke.
Past ash.
Past war.
Past past.
Though vile tempest within
Tattered and broken, I grin.
Past smoke
Past wretched and regretful past.
I will make the future last.
Reject both card and cash;
Make your dear future last.

Gray skies cover inns,
And restaurants as tame,
Never submit to those
Who want to be the same.
You're welcome.

My Madonna Is A Virgin

P ie ce s Of M yse lf

Shattered shards of me
Lie at my bloody feet.
They form a broken image.
I traipse blind from flame to flame,
Hungry blaze hunts my skin.
Burnt by others; engulfed
By my own cold sin.

The nacreous sky lies
Ethereal earthly task
Endlessly beyond my grasp.
Sometimes a star falls
And I enjoy splendor until it burns out.
But the sparks dry to drought.
The obsidian pieces of
A once proud figure
Slices deeply dying heart, dissipating hearth;
Sharpest stones blind eyes; reopen all scars.
I lie down and yearn for nacreous blue above
And yet it never comes.
Hurt ceases to hurt.
Heat ceases to burn.
The flame deepens its
Raw grasp, and yet,
The burns compound into flesh that stays.
I look gaze toward ground, down
At the cinders which lie
Under lazy and tired sky.
I am raw and intact,
Yet, upon nothing I act.

Let my words do what I didn't
Shards lie, the ash of doubt fills singed lungs
And my God-gifted heart rests none.
I am walking among the coals,
My body burns as mind becomes acidic.
And as the comets rise,
And a lone star falls,
And it only hurts,
And it only blinds.
Staring up
With wide eyes
Drawn toward cardboard sky
While the sun does not come.
But its flames graze me still.

Shards of former me scattered and dirty
I realized there may no longer be a 'me."
Feeble past conceptions of I
Rose in smoke to nacreous sky.

You're Not So Good, Either.

You Don't Have All The Answers.

HUMANITY DOESN'T HAVE TO
BE A CANCER.

The Giver

The giver
Sits and smiles.
A nacreous bed
I love to lay in
Always made for me
Of confounding color
She blinds me.
Pink tinge
Over the edge of forever.
Words whispered
In sequence divine.
Her edges smooth glazed
Meeting heaven with a glance,
Or a stare,
Or a gaze.
Starlit or sun-speckled
Always in sequence divine.
Her grace, embrace,
I want them all as mine.
And never would I forsake
Until I found—my giver
Only gives to take.

What a shame.
They only give to take.
It's all a twisted game.

Ativan

My brain is choked
But I have a plan
I can't move
But I stay calm
Because I know what's in my hand
Cars pass
The world turns
And time moves like sand
My heart falls to cinders
But the plan, oh the plan!
Pages turn
Struggles burn
But I do what I can
I look to nowhere
Nothing I see
To oblivion, I ran
I've executed nothing
Amounted to nothing
But oh, I have a plan
Milligrams
In my hand
Swallow Ativan

Cigar As Short As Life

One pill
Breathless
One more pill
Breath now still
One pillow with sheets
Worthless words
Hurtful things
Past everywhere
All the time, hunting me
Eyes, ears are much preferred to the void.
Silken hills,
Woolen coats;
Gold-plated clads my armor
For the cold mountain's ardor;
Futile.
My cigar's the size of life.
Then I light it
Eyeing those far-off hills of silk,
Only visible to God's eyes
Yet all I see ahead are lies.
Smoke and all
Still
Smoking quiet shrill
And the dirt stays dirt
And the Coyote hunts for kill.
Lonesome night I pray.
Please, hungry and despised feral One, stay alive—
Coyote, get the kill, eat your meal, go survive.

Dirt And Trees

Save me from me.
All out of luck
All out of love
Hills succumb
To rivers,
And the dirt
Sits and stirs.
Trees grow.
Tobacco surely burns.
Before my blood
Reaches the earth's care,
I have little time;
Not too much to spare,
I get a call
Daily from the pit.
But cigars are surely
Meant to be lit.
Withering wills;
Encroaching ills;
It's a pain to see.
But dirt and trees
Are surely meant to be.
Wings are born
As pairs of two.
I am learning flight,
But so are you.

And dirt and trees
Are surely meant to be.

Death grips
Death's wish;
Death has inevitable means
Life continues to
Split at the seams.
But dirt and trees
Are surely meant to be.
Gardens grow dormant
And mountains fade forever.
But dirt and trees
Are surely meant to be.

Surely they are?
Surely dirt and trees
Are forever engaged?

Surely
Trees
Need earth....
Surely... please,
I pray for ease.

But for the needy trees
Earth needs to receive.

Thunderstorms

Some people are like thunderstorms;
They cleanse the air
And are feared from below.
They cannot be touched—
Those thunderous people
Enter sky as enraged gray.
They may touch one, many, or none;
But few seldom struck more than once.
Fury from above heard by many,
They come and pass by quickly.
They stir the dogs
And rain on lone coyotes
Whimpering;
A reset.
You can hate the storm
And despise those stormy people,
But they're unable to hate you.
For it is above—
Those thunderous people,
Pure and ethereal,
And all too real,
Untouched and yet
All around and
Between past regret—
Just reigning
And only relenting
When they decide to.
Those thunderous few,
Though gray skies block blue;
Those people with storms

And fear and gray anger
And lightning and power
And fear and loathing dour
With sun as their backing—
Those people have power, for
Genius has no certain hour.
Genius only has flash then dies.
Genius only yells then cries;
Booms loudly and then recedes;
Shakes legs and weakened trees;
They needed to be cleaned.
I speak about genius, those thunderous ones—
Can you hear me?
Let the lightning be plentiful, then.
Let it strike dogs and weak men.
Let it kill all those who repent.
Let their bolt shock those who resent.
Genius comes; it destroys and then leaves.
Genius minds disrupt and disturb thee
For thunderstorms don't need belief;
They reign without license,
Unbothered by tiny creatures.
Genius revels in receding calm blue;
Thunderstorms rain and care none for you.

SAYSOMETHINGTHATMATTERS.

SAYSOMETHINGTHATMATTERS.

SAYSOMETHINGTHATMATTERS.

SAYSOMETHINGTHATMATTERS.

SAYSOMETHINGTHATMATTERS

SAYSOMETHINGTHATMATTERS.
SAYSOMETHINGTHATMATTERS.

SAYSOMETHINGTH

SAYSOMETHINGTHATMATTERS.

Nicoya

Ni co
Her eyes aglow
Beaming the light
From within her soul
Like perilous jewels
Of the softest blues
She may get carried and dragged
But she continues
To stride
With her head
Held high
And her feather-white hands
By her sonsy side

The transient vampires
Who've come
And gone
Detest her radiance
And are forced
To flee
From her daunting light.

Asphalt roads
Lay the canvas
For her chrome brush
And the sky
Is the showroom
For her winged chariot.
Her slightest smirk
Reveals

A slice of pink purity
In which
The vampires
Must divert
Their fickle eyes.

When she stumbles
She saunters.
When she mumbles
She serenades.
When she twitches
She dances.
Her beauty
Cannot be learned
Nor applied
Nor contrived
Ni co ya

Nicoya

Don't Love Her

Don't kiss her
Don't love her
Don't cry
Don't hug her
Don't give tears
No sorrow
She steals
Not borrows
Don't cry
Don't love her
Don't try
To touch her
Hold back kind words
Delete her number
Those eyes deceive
Her soul's deep slumber
Don't love her
Don't touch her
Please: no sorrow
You'll be better
Tomorrow
I promise
Please see past her
Don't lose rest
Talk to a pastor
She's not your best
Don't kiss her
Don't love her
The love you give
She'll take to another

So don't cry
Don't hug her
Don't tell her
You love her
Don't cry
Don't love her
Don't cry
Don't hug her
Don't kiss her
Don't touch her
So
Certainly, please
Don't love or hold her
Personally, I loved—
Deeply I told her
But not enough
My heart turned colder
So don't cry.
Don't cry
And don't kiss her.
Don't cry, though,
You miss her.

Poem 961

I often get lost.
Though I form a plan and route,
I am comfortable with doubt.

Sharp Pincers Of A Woman

Jumbled
Roses on the floor
Wilting in the cold
Petals melt to mold

Pincers for lips
My shell is hardened and black
Twig and horned legs
Humanity I lack

I crawl at night
Wake up when the pink smears sky dissipate in black
voids burning
I see no one outside, yet
My stomach roars churning.

Compound eyes seek onward
Only peeling and sucking young red
Only digging into skin
Only all want to be thin

But a bug can't sin.
A bug can't sin.

Father, don't forgive them,
For they know exactly what they do.

Please, Don't Love Her.

You know how this ends.

The scar never mends.

A Woman On The Road

Small and shallow breaths
Make for a shadow's sight.
But heaving her way through,
Overcame and took flight.

Gives with none
One of one
Stuck with the pain of life
Never numb

Always laughed
At the demon's gnash
Never scared
Despite painful crash

Gripping—
Dipping
Toward a plan.
Her eyes are fire.
Her skin is tan.
Her mode is go.
Supple as sand

The many monsters
Have reared their ugly heads.
The tires on her wheels
Have lost their precious tread.

And yet she drives.

All I See Turns To Brown

Sand stands
Apart from time.

It gets swept and kicked
But does not have a mind

It sits or stands
And takes shape in your hand.

Engulfing the world over
Whether sea or land.

It's permanence
Fades
Always.

Soulless Love; Two Dead Doves

It is always okay to weep
The tears help me to fall asleep

I am broken
I am the snake
Black heart in tow
Within I shake

Too heavy to walk
Too numb to cry
Too filthy to clean
Too young to die

I find no peace
The camera rolls on
And the paparazzi
Left me in a yawn

Every step in pain
For yonder days
Unknown strain
Unknown strays

Soulless love
Broken love
Clouds are only vapor mist paintings
The sun is a set of explosions
And leaves are nature's discarded carnage
And dogs are only loyal to their stomachs
Take me and eat me alive

But it rained and I miss Her

Her light made me see
How dark it's been
And how dark it is;
How dark it will be

Memories on the trip
I can feel good
Whenever I choose to
It's the heart of the Zulu

Death sleeps never
While Glory is fleeting
Obscurity is forever

Michaela

A glimmer among dirt
Yearned for a spark
Among dust they came forth
Cinders apart

Ash and steam
A hope and a dream
One touch; her touch
That's all I need

Space in between
Not much
For a love that lives
And loves to laugh

So what is space?
A minuscule thing
Breached by force
Of two hearts impure
Yet simple and clean.

Set in ivory skin
Two beaming discs of brown
When I gaze I stumble
Two beacons to burn
The shadows that shrill
And beg for mercy
From the light of her ways.

What better could she be?

What more could one want?
Practice may make purpose
But without effort,
So is she.

Every day you impress me to no end and make me
think that there could be so much more to life.
You're amazing, and the most amazing thing is that
you don't try. So many people love to do things, yet
you just love.

To the one who makes Beauty jealous and Fortuna
lucky: Michaela

Surely you could have stopped me. And surely I
could have left. But a sprout needs sun, water, and
breeze. So surely you were the thing for me.

Deep and abiding and two smiling eyes.
Scintillating across the sky; I looked up
And I saw why.
But all things are entropic.
A star burns bright and then dies.
Matter matters none. Time warps to planes
unknown.
But if all were shadow, I'd still know you, Michaela.
A light year across and I'd still see the figure of a
thing untold.
But all things fester in the dark.
All planes bend in time to the master of
Grandiose unknown, the father of all things.

And Hades waits in a dark kingdom. And stalactite Canines leer greedily at soft female flesh.

But I'd recognize you when hearts cease to beat. I'd recognize you when the soul meets untimeliest wound.

I'd see you through a mountain. I'd know you in complete dark. With you, every night is day. Surely, with you, death is not decay.

Wretched is the past. Michaela, you have what the countless stars plead for and what the night constantly stalks. But a moment is forever. And while a lamp bleeds its fleeting call, you are there to provide light.

Michaela.

T 341

Mirrors On The Floor

I make
People laugh
To see
A mirror
That smiles.

Shards broken.
I still see my reflection—
Cuts opened;
My redemption.

Mirrors On The Floor (Epilogue)

"And you don't understand why I gave this to you as a potential reference, still? Even after a second look?"

"Second look? I read it so many times—those nine lines—I treated it like a whole book."

"So you studied the poem, then; that's good. And nothing could be ascertained, try as you would?"

"I feel as though I understood it as deeply as I could. For a doctorate dissertation, I feel it's... not that *good*."

"And you dissected it head-to-toe—it's *whole* design?"

"It's on psychology; I only care for his mind."

"And so, I think you'd be surprised."

"Well, I guess I haven't seen any *lies*...."

"So what about Oliveri have you surmised?"

"Well, partial PTSD is certainly present in part."

"Is that not already a good start?"

"I think so—but that's all I've arrived at."

"Meaning what, to be exact?"

"It seems like his spoken shards of the poem refer to his fractured identity, the mirror in full being his past vanity."

"Good. That could be the case of Nick Oliveri."

"What do you mean 'could be?' I'm more interested in studies on PTSD."

"You read about him? His life and history?"

"Not necessarily."

"Did you search for verity?"

"I don't think so, candidly."

"Well, did you know he was diagnosed with Bipolar Disorder?"

"Oh... which one?"

"Bipolar One."

"Hm...."

"Maybe you looked at the poem like it was written for fun?"

"Not exactly… he was clearly a troubled boy vexed."

"Did you not research him for context?"

"Well, I analyzed the poem as best you told me."

"But not as well as I *taught* you, Bri."

"I could look into his biography… but I don't understand studying a dead male poet who didn't know anything about neuroscience—probably—to augment my dissertation on psychology."

"Well, just recite his last line."

"Okay, let me locate it this time."

"How does it go, Brianna?"

"You just want the denouement?"

"Precisely."

"'My redemption,' it says."

"Then what does that mean to your vocation?"

"Nothing for my dissertation."

"Look him up. Delve into podcasts and his own words. He was prescribed so much and survived from Ukraine."

"I will. But, in no way vain, I think he's—despite all I've learned—a bit insane."

"Hm. As is anyone who would publish a poem or story in that day and age. And yet, he is sort of a sage."

"I will scan every page. I will make my duty to study, despite his young age."

"No, no, his age is exceptional material."

"Then I will check out every serial."

"But didn't you see the PTSD and the distrust and the brokenness and the despair? It would be wise for you to analyze it."

"Oliveri's impaired, but since you advise, I will study every bit."

"It's not that deep, though. He makes jokes to see people smile, broken, yet finding identity."

"And so, you think he has PTSD?"

"It's for you to study and see."

Navel-Gazing Draft of A Dilettante

If you've never done anything
Or went anywhere
Or felt anything,
You can't write anything.

I Died

I died and went away for a while
For long I didn't stay
Long and only space
Longing for stark night
No matter longed for cold
Or feeling, or light,
Or anything in sight.
But nothing didn't exist in the cradle
Of the void where there was no "where"
And nowhere could I go;
Not there
Nor there

There was no "I"
After I died.

No matter how high you feel,
You can't escape.

The bone
So dry.
For sun then the dies
And when sunk void
Takes it all from you,
Be thankful.

Stay praiseful.

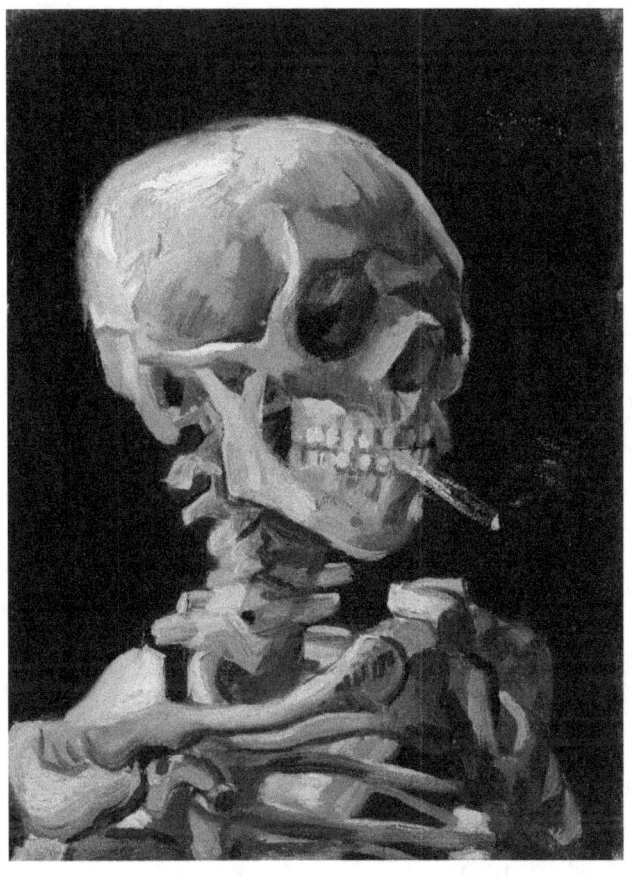

He Talks To The Page And It Listens

I'm in West Virginia or Virginia due south
To North Carolina, I'm losing
Gas and time and money, my mind.

I broke my mind again today.
Long stretch, cold road is why
I feel fortified to say
I'm mortified by life in ways—
My actions by fire among stars ablaze
Under lights, camera, my action's in poor taste.
And tonight I return to the sacred page
After I shattered my mind today—
Oh, God, I broke my mind again.
I broke my mind again today.
Oh no.

Crystalline, salient dreams
Cold breeze loud among silent screams
Those voices never relent
Though
You can change their sentiment
Maybe bleary night is highest time
To be most luminous
For even under collapsing sky
And stars sodden in relapsed black
There is a chance, although nigh,
That night is the time to shine.

Maybe alone you glow the brightest;
Maybe in scars, covered in callouses,
Broken mind, I told you shattered statuses
Many a night in one shadow,
And now I truly know—
That biting nights still yield moonlight
Despite a thousand lifetimes.
Warm-colored light
In dark sun's void for twelve to twenty
Never promised another twenty
Or one, even, as day is long and seconds waste
So today and tonight I don't expect the morrow
'Stead stay in warm light, cold night
Forget the sorrow
I walk on
And walk on
And I traipse and claw; I'm truly
On throat-dusted odyssey
Feet, please, don't fail me
Knees and twine of one branch
Wine aids tempest of purple sea
Please, feet, don't fail me
I'm merely a conduit to Nick Oliveri
World and earth like light drape true
I only have this page to talk to.

I only have this page to talk to.

I laid waste to past herds
Carcasses, now lasting dirt
And as I shatter again
My glue gets stronger

My shards get smaller
And I'll become what all beings be
Long after final breaths receive
Along shoreline and mad sea
Grains of sand are destined for me

But I just talk to a page
On behalf of Nick Oliveri
Who went too soon
And broke under few moons,
Many times too many
Rest in stolid life of any
Form of soul too restless
Thompson first said this:
"Too weird to live,
And too rare to die."
And so his soul forever
Nether-tied
But this about him remains true:
He only has this page to talk to.

I only have this page to talk to.

As Vonnegut Said

I searched my mind today
"Why do people cry?"
I got no answers
No true Science
They tell me to trust the answers
But I failed to get one
Why is it that tears fall?
Or why teary eyes fear none?
Or why bleary skies tear up?
Either way
The rain falls in the end
Either way
I'll never love again.
"So it goes"
As Vonnegut said.

I Drank A Painkiller

By the San Anton' river
I drank a Painkiller
Hot night quelled shiver

I smiled
First time
In a while

By myself;
Fatty liver;
By the river,
And it ran on
For seas larger
And more serene—
I dream.

Beautiful nightmares
In ninety degrees.
Drinking a Painkiller
Sitting by the river,
Still with my pain.
In ninety degrees,
At least it didn't rain.

Nothing's New

It's all been said
It's all been said
But not all is read
I stay behind
Take my time
Then I rush ahead
Nothing's new
All I see's red
Nothing's new
Nothing's new
It's all been said
Nothing's new
Who knew?

It's all been written
I spake, they took
They left, I look
To land far away
But'f I don't stay
I'll be like they
Who took and left
Left me bereft
And ran away
Laughing
There's nothing left to say
Nothing's new
It's all been said
Life rises renewed
From grateful dead
Lyrics

Write them
Sing them
Say them
Paint them
Spray them
Constantly
Novelty ends
All at once
It's all been said
But say it still
Forsake living will
Respect the dead
What to do
What to do?

Nothing is new, truly
But do it still
Though it's been done
Say it will
Overcome
After all
Is said
And done
Though it's been said before
No one else
Will care more
Than you
Nothing's new
Nothing's new
Except for you

Accept Yourself

Be cast out
Accept yourself
Get rejected
Accept yourself

Walk a lonely road
Find your audience
Confess your faults
Find your virtue

Fail and fall
Learn your next step
Trip again
Fail again
Success abounds

Be laughed at
Find joy
Be mocked
Find solace in yourself
Be mired in misery and indignities of all sort
And find the only one who can help you

The Orphan Part 1

Ostracized
There was never a knock
Though I loved the show
And everyone I know
There was and will be always
A simple silence to those crooked smiles
Sideways glances and giggles pointed
Alongside venomous words
And hissing murmurs about the orphan
Who wanted the world
Never expected to live more
Than a God-given year or so

And so I'm here still
Much to their chagrin
Maybe to yours
But I've gone on book tours
So fuck you
I've been to San Antonio
Traveled long to Chicago
I conquered great lengths
And now I laugh.
I remember the mockery
And now I laugh.
I recall the dark nights
Before and after the fights
Before and after the flights
In the dark and while the words
Caressed me in worlds absurd.

Oh, and she left me to die.
And she did too.
And she did too.
And she did too.
And she did too.
And she did too.
And she did too.
And she did too.
And she also did.
Now I expect it
And that one betrayed me
She also betrayed me
Yet, they all laid me
And that one flayed me
And
Yet
The hotter the flame,
The cleaner the soul;
The boy could not be the man
Without them leaving
All of them gone
For so long, seething
Salty waves drowning in deep lungs
Tears are tough when they come from slums
But I got by
No matter who left
I let the door open
And got raped
Worming fingers and tight crevices
Penetrated innocence
A girl's yelp
From an orphan

So many girls reddened by me
All of them left
By the dozens and more
But we will all die alone
I still hear their moans

I feel it right now
Or maybe a minute ago
But a minute is a lifetime
And life is but a second's time

And life is but a rhyme.
Kill yourself or carry on,
Uncaring is life's clock.
It ticks on despite your body
Live or dead or pale or shitting thin

Just live now, for worms will eat your skin

Decay
Decay
It's a shame

You hope, maybe a way
There's life beyond decay

Keep your faith.

Van Gogh

Life is only resistance.
It beckons persistence.

You've Been Lied To

Lies are only sold and stolen;
Women steal the lies
With their eyes to exist.
Men will buy them, too.
If you think that's at all sexist,
Then you've been lied to.
For the books and references
Falsehoods marker-made-plastic-paper-ink
As opposed to those
Written in stone
Now the children can't compose
In simple crayon strokes
They go on their phone.

And now we're collectively alone
Pharmacies take their bare-eyed share
Eyeing a Trillionaire's loan
As even they bow to masters unknown
As their furnace preys on innocent fear
We love those lies we want to hear
We love to hear that pills are kind
And syringes are for humankind
And now legally, tabs and needles
By every street sign
Watch your step, keep your view
But how do you see the truth
Or guard your heart,
If you know not what to guard?

Sanctity is not sacred

And you will never be sated
Off plastic pleasure and glass screens.

Men lie,
Women lie,
Numbers are false truths.
Numbers survey you;
Your every move and stride—it's true:
You've been lied to.

The Atlas Conundrum

I lifted up the world
And held it on my back
For a while it felt awesome
Then I started to crack
I did so much
Climbed great heights
I scaled many mountains
I slew dragons
I held the sun in my palm
I watched the world go by
On top of it all
I conquered what I could
I did what I had to
Often tired with no clue
But triumphant I stood
Medals and trophies and rings and belts
And such
It was all great
And I did all good
My achievements reigned for a moment
A bit of time went by, and I tired some
Then I stopped for a break, saintly
They asked, "what have you done lately?"
I did everything there was to do
Achieved great heights to applause
I sinned in grim dark and through dawn saintly
They ask, "what have you done lately?"

Poem 90

All the stars died. Stop me. Killing is indeed Murder.
Worship The Shepherd, not the herder.

I Saw A Dead Bird

I saw a bird dead today.
Not die, just dead.
In the air its feet lay.
On the concrete its head.

I will see the Phoenix tomorrow.
Imagine it proud and brash!
Its feet in full flight nay sorrow.
In flaming reflection I laugh!

The Heights

I have lived this life a rich one
I've given; I've been taken from.

I have tasted the richness of the rarified heights.
Within and outside myself, I have experienced glory,
true triumph.
I have climbed great peaks and looked down upon
humankind with laughter abiding by my heart.

But then I climbed yet further, further, to where the
air got thin and my feet became weary—this was
when I looked down and could no longer recognize
humans, their bodies, their buildings, or their way of
being. It all looked misty and myopic from way upon
peaks.
My lungs tired and thirsted for the damp air from
below. My weary feet bled and blistered. It was then
apparent that I climbed too high. But those peaks
impossible: I couldn't help but continue on my own.

This was up there on high:
Principles no longer applied.
Life was a joyous, hellish climb.
Full of thorns and predators,
And glistening grapevines.
If I ever said I was bored—I lied.
I was just dissatisfied
With the dirty air from below—
All the pettiness and fratricide.
So on my climb way past high peaks

Up above so high, my smile wry;
"I must have lived a million lives!"
So I got sick of the trees
And sick of the lies,
And I climbed so high
Past all mankind, until they
Could no longer be recognized.
So I stayed way, way up there,
And I died.

The Heights (Epilogue)

"Okay, so—thoughts?
Yes, Juan? Yeah, what did you think?"

"Wasn't he bipolar?"

"Okay, that's unconfirmed... but yes... his life and behavioral patterns would suggest he had a mental illness that would suggest fits of mania."

"So he was a maniac?"

"He was—well, more of a brainiac.... But, yes, a clinical maniac. And Tamara?"

"How could he be a brainiac by writing poems that I could write?"

"Well, there is to his words a certain bite."

"So, why are we reading this stupid book?"

"I want to know what you saw when you looked. Oh, Peter, yes—in the back?"

"I—I felt a little shook."

"Okay. So was it the hook?"

Silence the classroom took.

"Or was it something else? What did you feel when you went through it?
Yes, Peter?"

"I felt like it spoke to me a bit. I felt like it maybe...."

"Maybe what, Peter?"

"It teeters. I mean, it's like an animal with rabies. He's expressing something unseen like a baby. I haven't seen that kind of innocence lately. He's sort of brash while being stately."

"There may be a strain of dichotomy, indeed. So you're saying the poem is sophisticated while being a bit infantile?"

"Mm-hmm."

"Yes, Elisa? You haven't spoke for a while."

"I think he just sounds like loser. Anyone with the time to write all of this clearly has problems."

"Don't you think he's made amends?"

"What does that even mean, Amen?"

"I bet his parents drained all the water for their almonds."

"He sounds like a tyrant like Stalin."

"Are you saying Oliveri grew up rich?"

"Yes, and he was a bitch."

"Hey! Please keep those words out of class."

"What about the word 'ass?'"

"What about 'self-indulgent ass?'"

"That's enough, class! You need to participate to pass. Now, is there anything you took away from the poem's parlance?"

"It was sort of a dance?"

"Are you just saying that to rhyme?"

"No, I mean it split two emotions in short time."

"So, he *is* bipolar...."

"Weird."

"Was he white?"

"No way he was sober."

"I bet he sucked at poker?"

"Okay! That's enough…. In the last minute, write one sentence that best describes your impression of the lesson, or what you learned in this session."

One girl whispered to herself: "I feel like he beckons me."

"Here. Have a good weekend, Ms. Trumbly."

"Thank you. You as well; you enjoyed the reading today?"

"Humbly, I'll employ what he was seeing today. As soon as now, I feel like he spoke to me."

"Whatever."

"Oliveri was a loser."

"Bye, *Peter*."

"He teeters."

"Bye."

Laughter and teen shoes stampeded through.
None was crueler than the feet of humans clothed.
Tribes loved many, yet the lone one was loathed.
Classrooms are the new camps;
Diplomas are the new stamps.

I was met with contemptuous eyes

Yet, because of me, Circa is alive

Written Circa 2025

Nick Oliveri
All this fiction is fake, literally

Signed, Nick Oliveri

Circa was co-founded by me
Literally
Poems can't totally be told
Fictionally

You Don't Know Me

Life: I've loved what I have lost
The misery is such
That I feel no pain
I feel no pain
There is no pain
When I can smile in the snow
Or go for a walk alone
No cuffs, just tears;
Hallucinogenic zone.
It is a wonder that my eyes
Don't dry sooner
Maybe I have more to live
Maybe there is more to this
And hopefully I pray more to give
I stride, though I stumble
I spit, rage, trash-talk and mumble
Even at my lowest, I'm not humble

For I am weak
And reprehensible.
Not meek,
Not redeemable.
So I will stab and burn out and crash
And pick away at
The tender flesh of your inner soul
For time passed, my sins since swole.

Searching for life
Searching for more
There

Has
To
Be
More

And I'm greedy
And I'm a whore
People look at my eyes and jaw
Or cuts in soul; past thorns
But all they need to look for
Are my apparent horns
There is nothing left
There is no pain
Smiling through the rain
And for all time
Grin in the same
For I feel no pain
I'll laugh and cry
I'll learn and ask why
I'll venture and help
I'll take what's mine
I'll give what's mine
I'll laugh more
All the more I cry
And then to die.

Sweet dust tasteless
All your claims baseless

How can you know me
If I don't know myself?

With A Tear And A Pen

With a Tear and a Pen
He's already been carried off
She'd already been married off
Repented for the sins again
He'd already been labeled, "soft."
Soft and lost respect; new again
Tears dripped; he reached for a pen
Maniacally tired, diamonds dead
He cannot keep shining when
He sees her backside for the last time
Once-favorite pastime

The cold twisting air made him wheeze
And this was the great traveling wheel
Of life
Damn
Was he okay to trust?
Why was he not enough?
He yelled and had passion
But he could never be yet tough
To keep the respect of that
Perfect bride all white-laden
Even tears fall from a maven

An escapee from him
But she was her own woman
But also there was sadness,
If slavery is a choice,
Until you gain a voice.
Then why do we do this?

And live life full of fault and scammers
Liars thieve the joy of righteousness
But the weak get stomped on
And even the strong men
Get chomped on
Pushed aside and
Taken for an empty ride
It's all been said
And lived out.
Withering filaments in a broad chest....

But that bride;
That smile;
Those eyes;
You couldn't hide from them
They made you feel alive
And then you died.

Tell me I can't do it and I did it again.
Fuck! She told me we're better off friends
But if my girl leaves me then
My story won't end
The next one will end up
Being a ten
And then failure and tears
In the rain and the sin
And then the ending begins
And the distorted story's bent.
Now
The cycle brings the second coming
Churning that ever-eternal recurrence
And it starts

As soon as you incept
It becomes time to die
Snake's tail itself bitten
And the story begins
And the end is within.

Our failing eyes and
Through many tears we grin
Us men and us women
Let the story begin.
I stay to only write
With a tear and a pen.

Cold black night starless
In my asylum I run
Power is a cruel mistress

And the road is a battered whore
All I wanted was more—
Is that too much to ask for?

So I reached for the stars elusive
So lonely for naught it's been
I grasped for power and peaks
I hardly can cry, yet never Zen
I stretch for the past and friendly faces
I look for an ear lent
Stories to tell with a wide mouth
Rapid chatter of an acid tongue
Spittling vile of poison futures
Stolid pictures of what has been

But all I have is a tear and a pen
No one answers
No one belies my sage.
Alone
I sit and talk to my page.
Windows aged-black
Travelling knapsack
I talk to my page as one
With a pen and tear
For years, for years
Instruments and beers
I hurt, I hurt, they hurt, I hurt them
And now I'm left with page and pen.

I'm staged with rage and Zen
Bipolar page and pen
Killed a mage and many men
Hated boys and wait... women
Poems for movies, for then
Cinematic addicts
Blood from stones again
I did it all
Wine from water
Fatal cut soldered
Loved ones I've bothered
Chased off once bonded

A page is all I have to talk to
A pen is all the best I can do.

Talk To God

Oh,
The night is sweetest when day is longest
In solace with my wounds, dark night honest
Cold cover, no stars, and alone the strongest
No one to call, mate; unclear the time or date,
bleeding
Dull my words, too late, with none I commiserate,
feeling
The shroud of night
As it clutches tight

I can still recall
Those pills and white walls
But I sit hopeless, voiceless
The wind howls, screeches noiseless
So I listen to my own voice
Even when it seems pointless
But words spake from one to none
Echo louder than those voiceless ones.

So I talk to God.
These are my words:
"I sin, I cry, and I never learn."
I'm sure that was in Proverbs
Somewhere

Over the hills lie
Plateaus and open sky

A place beyond white walls and black windows

I try as a fly among black widows
Spindly, quivering legs and dead eyes;
They see everything, they know my lies
"I feel like I've cheated one hundred times!
Scientists don't believe in the Divine!
I'm a criminal, selfish and a swine!"
My voice breaks as I confess my crimes.
And why should I
Be loved by anyone?
I'm unlovable, futile, yet I reach for the sun.
Icarus shames me.
"Lord, I can't help but play with fire!"
Prometheus blames me.
"God, hear me!
Deliver me,
For my hope wanes."

Only tears remain
And when they run out
And then they dry on my face,
I enter a place
Gazing toward Heaven
But there's nothing in space
And then I grow weary, my feet sore from another
day
Monotony, vice, envy and spite

Spittle on my lips as I cry to the heights:
"God, save me. They want to bury me first!"
He replies with a verse
His response simple and terse:
"You cannot bury what came from the dirt."

"But it still must be my fault;
I disturb my friends and lose my lovers
My ventures end and failure hovers
My money is spent; I am life's blunders
Me."

It's always been me. My bad. My folly.
But then God said this to thee:
"I know you better, though you disappoint me. I
planted you a seed. I planned your trials to become a
tree."

So I talk to God.
So I wrestle with the powers that be.
He's my refuge, though I hate authority.
So I talk to God.
I wrestle with thee.
At least
He hears me.

They All Left Scars Leaving Me; Ahahaha

Buried
Underneath her cards
Her love notes and pictures
Are the purple bottles
And loveliest scriptures
Underneath her hairpins and triggers
Her brushes and clothes and
Photos from dinners
Are buried bottles amber
Sacred scriptures
Because what once was lost
Is still lost; gone from me
Now all I have are those pictures
But more vital: those sacred tinctures
Hidden away, please, no more pain
But all those prescriptions
Are all that remain
I found myself after breaking mirrors
In shards on the ground;
A shattered image
Of a man once a boy
With dreams and provisions
Lost what he had
Except for his vision
But I'm sorry to say
It's muddy and gray
Pills white as snow
Purple poison breaks the day

Amber bottles pile and grow
There is less of me now
Just, please, no more pain
That joy and my glee
She took it from me
Now all that remains are piles buried
Underneath the pictures long past
Feed me the prescription
That scripture flag half-mast
Piles of memories
Far flung, we traveled sea-to-sea
But those love notes are paper
Those pictures are flat, I see
And now I realize, finally
That the one I loved was me

Welcome To The Jungle Part 2

Welcome to the Jungle.
No one will come to save you
But someone is sure to get you
They bare sharp teeth and black eyes
They have lawyers and papers
On their side silken ties
They smile and guffaw true
As they come to imprison you

No one inclined to save you
And, wanting more than a few—
They're out for flesh to chew
And bring you to a grave or prison
Between white walls or heavy tall-
Walls of debt with no one to call

Your time has come
There is no one
Dying echoes in night;
No stars; dying trees;
Only coyotes
For no one—it's true—
Will come to rescue you
No one will save you
Floating in the abyss
Alone in the jungle
Pairs of red eyes exist
Many blinking from behind
Where fangs and venom hide
It is a lonely walk with

Danger as a sole ally
No rules does jungle abide by
For there is no pride
In eating other humans
As a human
No dignity to be found or felt
In convincing a wolf to part with pelt
Blood tastes delectably
On a stomach so empty

No one has pride
No dignity; empty eyes wide
And black and pale skin and
Yellow teeth on green tongue
Once humans, now don hide

Lions have the only prides
Multitudes spread far-flung
If only you'd join one

But you don't belong there
You don't belong anywhere
So no one to the rescue
Maybe,
Only
You can save you

Welcome to an easy death wish
In the script, you were born for it
Life's a mere gap between dips.

Laugh At The Void

Laugh at it:
The void.
Treat it with scorn
Don't respect the void,
For in it, you were born.
You make sacrifices, feeling torn
Between two paths, each two more
They spring onward, a maze-like chore
Dizzy head and tired legs—
It gets darker yet

Though you don't know
Your life's been sacrificed,
Sold to the highest bidder.
Through the forest's woes you walk
Though the trees get thicker and thicker.
The smoke stays gray, no more streets
As your path gets slicker.
And your pockets empty as your lungs cave in
Though your spirit's all the richer

Hope grows dim
The light narrows thin
But you still hope that
The sun warms the morrow.
Calloused hands clasped, you pray
For just one day without sorrow.
But those stars in the sky
Are just goblin eyes
Staring down forever;

The only sound you hear
Are cackles and howls
Twisted creatures and hungry hounds
As the shapes flicker, a whisper:
"They only want you."
Alone is it, for there is no room for two.
You recall the days when sky was blue
But the sky is dark
The air is cold
The road gets long
The tale is old

Back When I Was Healthy

We laughed a lot way back when I was healthy
Not the meek; the world is given to the wealthy
Way back, when I needed not pills
Only her warmth stopped the chills
The wind blows cold to bone to bone to bare trees
Yet the breeze warmed calmly when
I was your only seed

Testaments burned and scriptures turned
Now prescriptions alone left in the urn

Searching for a spark and kindle
Ashes to ashes, hills of dust I trample on
From endless ruin, melting clocks, I ramble on

Eyes of flame made for sunny days
And over time the sky's shining light,
Cruel eye,
Turned my face and spirit weathered
The sun scorched all to dead desert
Now I search on toward forever lands
Fighting on toward nether worlds
Hoping to find Valhalla
But for now, faded brown
Blackened ash, hollow crown
I trek as my sins come back sad
You were all I needed
Now horizon's all I have

Back When I Was Healthy
(Epilogue)

Gasp
Take in the ash
Now my lungs are black
Grasp
At tomorrow
Now I walk
Along time borrowed

Fading oil painting of her face
Timid vignettes full of fear's embrace
I was healthy back then
But the memory never fades

"He's a loser trying to be, like, dramatic."

"He's using you, Michaela, to be emphatic."

".... Yeah.... I guess."

"You don't miss him, do you?"

"No. Of course I don't miss him. Why would I?"

"Good for you, babe."

"Yeah, good for you, Mick. You're a queen and did all you could."

"Yeah, I don't miss him. I, I never would."

"Girl, as you should!"

The Coyote

We laugh like coyotes howl
Because we are just as foul
And because we need to.
Because desire is innate
And we love what we hate.
The mangy coyote
Is all alone too
In the cold and snow
And it howls like you.

Have you ever slept alone?
Or been without a home?
Have you ever gone hungry
Among bare branches,
Under no starry night?
Have you been scorned?
In life, lived in fear?
Have you been hated?
Mistrusted?
Have you ever felt sated?
Wintry nights alone
Like the coyote hated?

You laugh in pain
And howl in vain.
The coyote does too.
The coyote is like you.

The Orphan Part 2

I've been thrown away
Abandoned and let go of
Ostracized only because
I was not like them
And I never could be

I spit on the ground
I cry but I don't care
I threw up on them
And I didn't care
I called them dumb pricks
And I didn't give a shit
For I am an orphan
I don't mind and I swear
I am an alien
And
As an alien should
I abducted them
And they were all entranced;
To my tune they all danced
Groups of faceless beings one
Mocking me and ripping me
I felt the salt in my blood
Gravel is sand
And sand is for beaches;
I play the clown
The painted face with a plastic smile
Estranged from the smiling crowd;
I control still the hearts of that town
And I brought them to concealed frown

Made green memories for all around
Forever
I live
And they fade
And they're nothing
For new bride and groom caught my vomit
Their new-born baby forever stained bonnet
My genetics are laced within their sonnet

They all left within my mind
A place I stay for long, though
It dispels me in short time

Yet they cast me out

They disposed of my face
And have forsaken my name
Yet I am the greatest they graced
Though I cry after they take;
I created then they took;
I made them drinks; they drank and looked
I walked with my own shadow
I took a pictures that fade now
They kept
I roamed the hazy streets
Walking along endless concrete
I shed tears when my city was bombed
All I got was a stale "sorry."
And they strode right by me

Goblins mirroring each face
Had no rules but to castigate

The weird ones
The creeps and the teary suns
From homes broken and bombed
On my shoulder I carried tons
And tons

And tons

And tons more to break me again
It seems I'm from another planet
They walked away
Like when I was born
Just as when I made a company
Just as when my sums were many
By myself
The voices of vice echoed within

I went to the Grove
They misname me
I go to the Louvre
Disdain for me
And Wicker Park
And the Riverwalk, too
Noah would deny me from his ark
As the rain poured with death around
They would mock me as they drowned
But a cigar's wisp in night
Stayed the sweetest sound
And they still mocked me
And they didn't want me
From the place that didn't want me
From the place that didn't want me

From that place that couldn't keep me
And now I can't go back
No matter the warm touch of sun
I wouldn't mind the clouds of home
But there is no home
After sprouts showed; I roamed
They have no room for an orphan
No space for the unwanted
No home for the unvaunted
I cried alone oh, oh
So many nights ripe
With empty stars I couldn't reach
My eyes wiped
But they didn't like how I was weak
Or that I was weird
Or something about my beard
Or my eyes they couldn't contain
Or maybe I'm a narcissist
Spending time to tell my pain
But maybe you can relate
But I might not care, for
I might be one of them:
Humans, creatures
I just make features
Which you read now
While they fake happiness
It is a heart I endow
Maybe somewhere
If only
If only there was a willing ear
If only I could stop from the tears
Go and date the dry-eyed

That's them;
I'm me
I stay impossibly myself
I roleplay as an Oliveri
And I paint what you will see;
Pictures of a lone person
Lusting for evergreen spring
Slow and traipsing lowly
Mindlessly distilling
The nature all around me
Finding more of what could be
I reach
For what
I want, see:
No matter how many mock me
It is I who sincerely sees me
And I know my desire truly
I just hope no one gets killed
I hope the sun rises again
And the dawn is painted gold
Dusted in pink and powder blue
And that one day,
Maybe,
I meet You.

You.
But I doubt whether you exist.
You.

Maybe
I meet You.
The First of February

Is the day I speak true

I pen this Today
Fired at by dismay
Rained on by rage
The breeze is harsh but the cold keeps me numb
The sun is stout, but hallucinations
From dehydration are fun

Those hallucinations
From dehydration
Dry and tired ventilation;
Hallucinations
Are one's fun as
Reality is only violations

Strictly

The truth lies in the middle
Democritus' imagination
Down to the smallest grain
So we can't see, eyes do little
For mystic gains in desert

Mirages cope
Strictly
A hope
Of Democritus

But speculation and science cannot cure loneliness.

My Favorite Day At Night

"I just need to know... what's going on in that
beautiful brain of yours?"

The car whirs.
My hand covers hers.
The night is bright.
The top is down.
Her top was too.
Waistband now;
Once red gown.
Her black hair down.
Her pillow lips,
My sanctity.
A long part of me held the simple urge
To express my bleak true love for her

But she just laughed and looked ahead.
Maybe my question was in her head.

"You laugh. What's going on?"

"I don't really know what you mean."

"Everything you say is like a dream.
And yet, I feel like you hold back.
You have so much going on up there.
I'd love to have your thoughts fill the air.
If you're sad, I'd love to hear your pain.
If you struggle in sleep, I'd share your nightmare."

"That's really nice of you to say. Sometimes I get lost in my thoughts, I guess."

I tried to slow down
But the tires kept racing
Toward her house.

"If there's ever anything on your mind,
I'd love to hear it."

We approached her street.

Our hands parted.
Our heads met last.
That was my favorite day.
I watched her walk away.

Plastic Wristband

I was down and out
They pegged me as depressive
Little did they know
That I was more than that

I was suicidal and
In wheelchair with a wristband
Imagine how my parents felt
Watching me roll away

I felt the screams of a life
Controlling me

I wanted to scream
Yet my lips stayed pursed
I was told "bipolar"
They said my mind was cursed

They stuck me in white walls
Group therapy never
Did a thing for me

I'm bipolar and now I always win
I'm bipolar, now I always sin

So laugh at me
Stage a couple chuckles for the theater clown
And cackle at the funny face;
The fool donning oversized frames
Vivid colors round his neck

Scarves and handmade shoes
Silly kerchiefs and tacky patterns
Laugh, mock the clown, guffaw
He is a mirage they saw
Just things to show
Another figure to view
But the clown can see all of you....

For I was born into the rough
But always with a birdie on tee
Now regrets, like air, haunt me
Now I subside in fantasy
Living a life in mine own from reality

Bipolar, what a fantasy

I'm gifted and I shifted
I got my mind never on
But the doctor's never wrong, right?
So now I'm staged for a villain's song
The cops are never wrong, right?
In the din,
Dim light quivers.
I was told that I'm gifted
I was told my eyes were bright
I was told I'd go places,
Then I did.
I was told I would reach great heights,
Then I did.
Teachers are never wrong, right?

But maybe I'm here for a real reason

Maybe I'm a gift to those who never could
Maybe I'm made to commit treason
A sacrifice to the Lord
A pageantry for the gods
Maybe I struggle and could never be good

Maybe I'm a joker in the poker deck
Perhaps I hide the aces
To myself I keep the faces—kings and queens
Maybe a whole deck up my sleeve
Maybe my words don't mean what I said
Or I give everything I ever meant

I don't mean to disguise
Thin pillows in dark nights
Barred windows small
Embedded in vast white walls
The solace never came, no sun
Only my parents would come
To see me in the hospital
I don't have the strength
To laugh at the tragedy
Of Kierkegaard's angst

Some inexplicabilities
Cannot possibly be smiled at;
Some frigid eternities
Cannot be for long survived.
Imagine frozen creatures still, once alive

Maybe an explanation exists somewhere
As dim light quivers

Maybe there is a waning cloud willing
To open its mouth
Maybe

I swear

I swear I don't hate people
And I don't want violence
And never meant wrong
Despite adversaries and
Their snakelike silence
There's more to the story

Have faith in me and have faith in God
God will only help you after death;
But I will carry you far
On dirt, 'til death, no rest

Legalistic Christians
Atheistic visions
Dim light quivers
Only I make incisive inquisitions

You are all nomads
And think you have a home
Who really is the clown?

I swear I'm better off alone
For a monster is a monster
I was born as such
I was born in the grotesque when
Gothic pictures were fairytales

Chernobyl was Disney World
It's about dark morning
And I write in this moment such
I am in time with the Dutch
Fuck a Ukrainian
They call me Tasmanian
I'm a Devil tiny teeth and eyes
Growling, devouring mink
Sharpened stalactites
Scratching and hurting because I can
You're weaker than you think
You reside in quicksand
A dim light quivers
Your country shivers in dark
Reigning over nothing

But who am I to speak on people
And their given differences
Except for that
I granted them their skin
I gave you all eyes to see
And minds to read, as well
As these words to save you

But as you were never asked
When you wanted to be born,
You won't be asked
When you'd like to die.

You live as if
There is only light forever
As your bones grow old

Skin sags and mind slows
Then bullet or bus strikes
Now, there is no more light

But I remember those white walls
That wristband cut deeper
Than any handcuff could
The plastic colder than any metal

I couldn't see a starry night in my asylum.
The bars on the windows stole moon's glimmer.
The pillows thin held my grimace
The weak sheets soaked in tears
There couldn't have been a deeper cave
Nor was there ever a broader trial
Than those black nights
White walls confined

My roommate in the asylum was nice
He wore glasses and
Shared my same wristband
I could feel the weight of his small smile
He worried about his job and tried to hide
The anxiety in his eyes
But like me,
He was institutionalized
Like me,
He wanted suicide

But there was a ray
As I saw him trying
To get along some pace

I never talked to him after I got out
I hope he's not dead
He was almost as young as me
He still had some filament within
He searched for it among the dark
Though the light grew ever dim
There was still some flicker within

I hope he found it
I hope I didn't snore too loudly
I hope, to him, I didn't come off too proudly
After all, when all becomes sand
We both wore the same wristband

God Bid Me Live

I dragged aimless
Shameless night
Only sleep was painless
Then I couldn't sleep again
Time for more medicine
But I fell especially hard today
The tears never heavier

He commanded, "don't come to me yet."

"But I seek death," I said.
"And I'm beyond upset.
I can't
Take
One
More
Step.
Please, God, I want death."

"No," he whispered. "Now is not your time.
You will live! You will be more. For, you have
More to give."

"I don't feel it, Father. I have nothing left. Drunk on
tears. High on vitriol. I feel already
I've seen it all."

But the sun stunned wintry crystals
Alone but together with all,
God bid me live.

I wanted to die; no more is in this!
But I didn't have a say in it.
I looked up to open sky
More colors than had met my eye.
And to think, one second ago
I wanted to die.
It occurred to me, that moment in time:
I have more to suffer, what a thing!
I have more to bring
I have more to fetch
More lonely nights
More sickness to fight
More gifts to offer
More laughs to crack
More times to bite my tongue
Or to eat a tasty snack
And next time I'll savor every bite
I no longer want to end it
I'll say yes to all rejection
And consider all conceptions!
I'll rattle off my best
I'll fail many more a test
I'll care a little less.
And maybe,
Though
I cry now,
I might soon smile for a change,
Or maybe help someone do the same.
Maybe these tears aren't all
In
Vain

God bid me live
I didn't want another breath
Yet I had no choice
But to dodge death.
God bid me live
He commanded me so;
The sun shone through snow
Bright crystals glistening
Peaks of horizons listening.

I thought it was my last day to live
But I was told I had more to give.

I wished no longer to carry on and live
But God spake and said I had more to give.

I thought of traffic, pills, wine, guns or knives
Yet True God bid me stay alive

Now I'm still here as of 2025

God bid be stay alive

I pleaded for an end
Wanting only to die
But God bid me stay alive

Those wintry crystals cold
Met with sun so warm
Made so much sense in woods lost
Therefore in highest time of fight
In greatest time of strife

Even though I had sinned
God told me I had more to give.
He said, "Go live."

More Works By Nick Oliveri

The Conjurer (Bestseller)

Monsters In My Mind (Bestseller)

Becoming The Conjurer (Bestseller)

The Last Conjurer (Bestseller)

Oxycodone And Her Canvas

A Letter From The Conjurer (Bestseller)

Her

A Genocide Too Small

A Boy Just Like Me

Author Bio

Nick Oliveri is a Ukrainian-born #1 bestselling author and fashion designer. He is often dubbed as a controversial creator of transgressive fiction and genre-bending literature.

Nick plumbs the depths of the human psyche in his fiction, sharing his potent tales of tragedy and triumph with the world. Skilled at crafting sentences that bring his characters and their narratives to life, he is passionate about the beauty the written word has to offer.

Oliveri draws from a unique set of creators that have inspired him throughout the years. These include Jean-Michel Basquiat, Vladimir Nabokov, Stephen King, Lil Wayne, and Hunter S. Thompson.

Nick is a startup co-founder dedicated to the onset of the circular economy. Born in Ukraine but having grown up in the United States, today you can find Nick next to nowhere, and sometimes somewhere, enjoying whatever it is that he does.

Do you not see the children on a stick?
We are not too far away from this.

OFFICIAL ENDING

The end. Shun yourself.
Nothing in you is worth even pity.
Poison yourself.

This is the end.
It has been my ends.

Real meaning means not.
Don't respond;
'Tid be all for naught.

I'm sick and dying
With no one to drink with
Crying
I am sure that those who left me
Guffaw at such vulnerability.

We're all going to die; surely this is basic?

Bring me all the cases, you lost ones.
I welcome you and you to try me first.

But you cannot bury one from the dirt.
You cannot make purely sanitary
One who is interplanetary.

Good luck, strident men without law.
Bring me war, you lawyers without cause—
I bring warriors and unsheathed claws
Come find me, message me, sue and serve me;

I care not for a clause.

You'll gasp as blood floods your lungs
As my threats are not permissible in court
And I do this for sport.
I have so much more to say.
Stay tuned.

A wing sprung from springtime young
A dark age ended with sip's poison tongue

Try and gather thee
If that is,
You can catch me
Tiny men in ties (lawyers, attorneys)
Be Pushkin's scrapped treatise

I know you don't understand.
You'll never know or have a hand.

Don't reach out to me.
I have PTSD.

You can't negotiate with death.
I assume you value your breath,
So stay away.
Yamaka. Kufi laggards. Papacy's braggart.
From everyone I steal.
I'll fictionally kill you (legally and for real).
Flaccid fat secular Jews; broken Sharia rules;
Predatory Catholics die alone out of view.
Desperate women's whims

But if I mention 'men,' there exists bias?
What of both; men and women—
Is it not all for sin?

UNOFFICIAL ENDING

Whatever I may do next,
Think of as an experience
What I just performed
You experienced
Think that you're delirious
Think as long as you like,
But you cannot think what you want.

I could do anything next
And I will do it all

Ita Volui
Believe me

Best always,

Nick Oliveri

A mess always,

Nick Oliveri

Traveling tumbleweed with no intent;
Achieving aims heaven-sent,

Nick Oliveri

P.S.
If you put my head on a stake,
Then a martyr you do make

Dearly,
So this message is to Atheists, too,
Sincerely,
Agnostically,
I try to convince, but for most it won't work;
Yet if I end up killed, would you become a convert?

Ontological things don't matter much to me.
There is a song in my soul; I think I just sang it.

You, reader, act *so* sly
But you were born to die

Among the many of lesser ilk
You drink from the Lower's milk

The sun shines
And earth dries

Die again.

You can't.
Not guilty.

I'm not guilty
I'm not guilty.

I'm guilty.... No. I misissspsoke—
I'm not guilty.

But how do I plead, again?
You may have to read again.

What did I say in that part back then?
Which school of thought did I attend?
You may have to read it all again.

Which school of thought did I attend?
You may have to read that again.

Render me useless.
Please cast me aside.
But if you're reading this line,
Then in me do you abide.

I swear I'm not manic or,
At least not currently.
Right now I'm in Brooklyn
Dimly lit and nylon strings
Reverberate
A dim and dispassionate night
Warmth in late winter's delight
I no longer long for Spring
For there is a new horizon new renewed along
This course toward the sun for,
Even if I am destroyed or,
Something worse before budding Spring
Nothing yet has defeated me and sure,
I don't say this maniacally;
As though I sin and travel alone along grim
Turns in, I write this at night in Brooklyn.
I swear there is hope catching horizon;
I swear I feel the early dawn's drip;
I hear silent quakes of prairie's dew;
Intimated me and you;
Not indoctrinated; serving you

Now I write this on the road again.
I swear on every soul of Man.
There is no 'you', only I;
And there is no 'we' in life's grand sigh,
Only goodbye.